Intimacy with

GOD

AN INVITATION TO PRAYER

SIMONE MULIERI TWIBELL

THE FOUNDRY
PUBLISHING®

978-0-8341-4180-3

Printed in the
United States of America

Cover design: J.R. Caines
Interior design: Sharon Page

Library of Congress Cataloging-in-Publication Data
A complete catalog record for this book is available from the Library of
Congress.

The internet addresses, email addresses, and phone numbers in this book
are accurate at the time of publication. They are provided as a resource. The
Foundry Publishing does not endorse them or vouch for their content or
permanence.

10 9 8 7 6 5 4 3 2 1

To the memory of Andrew Twibell, the mighty warrior, whose life of prayer in the midst of a fiery furnace proved to be the greatest invitation of his life.

And to my twin sister, Aline Mulieri, who has continued to smile in the midst of a seemingly insurmountable battle.

✳ CONTENTS

❋ INTRODUCTION

I have wanted to write a book on prayer for a long time—perhaps because it would incite me to reflect even more on the importance of this subject or perhaps because it would remind me of the constant blessings that prayer can reveal. As I thought more about it, however, it dawned on me that it would be simplistic to attempt to write on this topic as a merely academic exercise to stimulate and provoke critical reflection on the topic with the goal of motivating individuals to engage its practice. My intention here is much broader: not only to provide a careful presentation of the *dimensions* of prayer but also to attest to the *privilege* and *promise* of prayer with the hope that many will discover its *power* anew.

I was born in Brazil, a land that attracts thousands of visitors to its shores. One of its most visited places is *Cristo Redentor* ("Christ the Redeemer"), a statue that stands high on a hilltop overlooking the prosperous and magnificent landscape of Rio de Janeiro, one of Brazil's largest cities. With outstretched arms,

Cristo Redentor welcomes all visitors alike. The view from the mountaintop is truly breathtaking and awe-inspiring, drawing individuals from all over the world to capture its strikingly scenic sights with photographs and videos that will be ingrained in their memories for years to come. It is interesting to consider that, if one were to climb over the other side of the mountain where the statue is located, one would actually see the whole picture of the place where *Cristo Redentor* stands—and not just its attractive side. Right behind the statue, the fragile shacks of the poor stretch for miles into the distance, deprived of the glorious paradise that tourists come to observe and admire. On one side, beauty. On the other side, heartbreak. And this is the reality of any life and every place. We cannot walk for long in the streets of a city without encountering elements of beauty and elements of tragedy, meandering side by side even when they might refuse to walk hand in hand.

Prayer has often taken a similar path, separating beauty and tragedy in its evocations. We pray with joy in our hearts when the winds of life are in our favor and with cries of sorrow when they are against us. In this book, I suggest that prayer should embrace joy and sorrow, praise and pain, beauty and tragedy—all within the same breath. Life is not sometimes beautiful and other times painful. It is always beautiful *and* painful. So, as we learn to pray unceasingly regardless of our circumstances, we do so remembering that God is also praying *with* us. When we engage in the act of prayer, we join the Suffering Servant, our risen Lord, who prays *for* us so we may rediscover the beauty of his glory as we remember his nail-pierced hands. Prayer is an invitation to come alive through the Spirit of God who intercedes *through* us and helps us envision new possibilities in the midst of our human impossibilities. Prayer, in a nutshell, is a response to the grace of God already at work in us.

As a partnership between the human spirit and the Spirit of God, prayer is a two-way street. It is sharing our most sacred desires, deepest longings, and heaviest burdens as we are guided back to the paths of self-discovery by the Spirit of God, to examine ever more carefully our desires, longings, and burdens. At its most fundamental level, prayer is an act of worship, and every act of worship strengthens our spirit. At its most practical level, prayer is an act of obedience, and every act of obedience strengthens our will. At its most realistic level, prayer is an act of trust. We trust that God is there, that he hears our prayer, and that he knows how best to answer. Every act of trust through prayer strengthens our faith. For these reasons, prayer carries the seed of hope as we travel though arduous wastelands and sun-scorched earth. Prayer also carries the sound of silence as we journey through long, twisting, desert-like roads. Prayer is kindled by the glare of light as we encounter dark tunnels, dead ends, and turnarounds along the pathway of life. Finally, prayer is deeply grounded in the love of God, who invites us to embark on the many unpredictable sailings of life, led by his always present, never failing, overly abundant love.

Some remarks regarding the structure of this book are necessary. Any attentive reader will observe that this book is divided into three parts. I have intentionally divided it following a Trinitarian approach to prayer. Although this categorization is certainly not the only way to understand the dimensions of prayer, it is representative of the role each Person of the Trinity plays in the life of the believer as we pray. **Part I** deals specifically with the unique contribution of contemplative prayer as we learn to honor and enjoy the presence of God the Father. Because prayer seeks connection with God, those who pray must learn to center their attention on God's presence. But prayer does not only seek to establish a connection with God; it also seeks to recruit his intervention on earth. As such, **Part II** addresses the role, ministry, and opportunities of intercessory prayer based on the model of Jesus Christ, who made supplication for us while he was on earth and lives even now to intercede for us. Because prayer in this form is an act of supplication, it agonizes over the hardships and sufferings that characterize our lived experience on earth, seeking the aid, direction, and consolation of God at every turn. Finally, as a two-way street, prayer must learn to listen to the voice of

God in order to receive direction, blessing, and guidance for our lives and the decisions we make. In this lifelong process of learning to hear and discern the voice of God, the primary goal is to remain open to the Holy Spirit and recognize the Spirit's voice with its many inflections. Therefore, **Part III** invites us to learn and discover the many ways God speaks so we may learn to be guided by his voice in its many inflections.

In my own journey with God, I have learned a few things, and I hope to share some of those lessons in this book. When I was a senior in college, I came across invaluable books that taught me the way and value of prayer. As an international student, I did not have the resources to purchase these books (or any book, for that matter), but I discovered we could get books through interlibrary loans, a free service the library provided that allowed us to renew them up to six months! And that is how I became immersed in a world I never knew existed: the writings of the mystics and heroes of the faith who helped me understand the depths of prayer. I became acquainted with Francis de Sales, Teresa of Ávila, Madame Guyon, François Fénelon, Brother Lawrence, Thomas à Kempis, William Law, Thomas Kelly, Rees Howells, and many others. In my mind, these individuals were spiritual giants who—despite the fact that they lived in contexts of great struggle, political unrest, tragic loss, and social deprivation—learned to live holy lives made possible by the love of God. Their writings made a huge impact on me, and I have tried to implement some of their wisdom in my own life.

Prayer is simple. Prayer kneels when life gets hard, stands on God's promises when life seems uncertain, and enjoys the gifts of God when all seems just right. As a senior in college who desired to know God, one thing became evident: if I wanted to learn more about God, the best way was to *know* God. It would have been a mistake to sacrifice the actual experience of God on the altar of intellectual curiosity. Experience and knowledge complement each other—neither should be sacrificed. Similarly, in order for us to learn about prayer, the best way to do that is to pray. A few suggestions can help us learn to become better at it, and that's what I hope to offer in this book. I am afraid too many contemporary books on prayer present it as a "strategy" in order to experience something other than what prayer is meant to be. Prayer is neither magical nor mechanical. It cannot be reduced to a set of principles or utilized as a strategic plan for some ulterior or utilitarian purpose. Prayer is both a discipline and a work. And it is often hard work.

During the many years of my life when heartbreak and loss reminded me of the fragility of life, I discovered that God is still actively restoring, healing, blessing, and re-creating beauty in this world, which is partially made possible by our response through prayer. As we respond to God's invitation to walk with him side by side, hand in hand—especially when we might not feel like it—we discover that God can turn every difficulty into a blessed opportunity as we pray. The invitation is open. The journey into the depths of prayer might prove to be one of the most profound invitations we receive on this side of eternity. I hope you decide to take up the challenge.

PART I

CONTEMPLATIVE PRAYER

"Turn to the Lord with your whole heart, let him be the most important part of your life, and your soul will find rest. If you put God first, you will see his kingdom blossom within you, for the kingdom of God is living in peace and joy with the Holy Spirit, a thing given to those who do not yearn for him with all their hearts."

—Thomas à Kempis, *The Imitation of Christ*

※ ※ ※

"Listen to your soul as it says, 'I am *willing* with all the power of my being that the desire of God be accomplished within me. I am *willing* to be here, ceasing from all my activity and all of my power, so that God might have his desire of fully possessing me.'"

—Madame Guyon, *Experiencing the Depths of Jesus Christ*

※ ※ ※

"The way of prayer is not a subtle escape from the Christian economy of incarnation and redemption. It is a special way of following Christ, of sharing in his passion and resurrection and in his redemption of the world. . . . The way of prayer brings us face to face with the shame and indignity of the false self that seeks to live for itself and to enjoy the 'consolation of prayer' for its own sake."

—Thomas Merton, *Contemplative Prayer*

1 ❋ FROM THE SHALLOWS TO THE DEPTHS

We encounter the presence of the Father on earth in many different ways. We get glimpses of God's character by observing nature. We also discover his attributes through the smiles of children, the embrace between an older couple, flowers as they wither in winter or bloom in early spring. If we are attentive to our surroundings, God's presence can be felt and observed almost anywhere, for God is everywhere at all times at any given moment. But apart from nurturing a meaningful relationship with God, these sporadic encounters would be devoid of permanence—not because God would choose to purposefully hide his presence but because we are not thoughtful and attentive enough to see God in the mundane aspects of life.

It gives me great assurance to know that even before I ever entertained the thought of seeking a relationship with God, he was already seeking a relationship with me. God longs to make himself known and is always pursuing fellowship with

God's children. God's pursuit of us precedes our finding God. In fact, God placed a longing in our hearts so that when we found him our relationship would be truly reciprocal, even if it remained unequal. Augustine of Hippo captures the essence of this intricate relationship with these poignant words in his famous *Confessions*: "Despite our lowness, human beings aspire to praise you, though we be but a particle of your creation. You awake in us a delight at praising you. You made us for yourself, and our heart is restless until it finds its place of rest in you."[1] The rest every restless soul longs to find can be appropriated only by the continual cultivation of a life of prayer. American Trappist monk Thomas Merton said, "Prayer begins not so much with 'considerations' as with a 'return to the heart,' finding one's deepest center, awakening the profound depths of our being in the presence of God, who is the source of our being and our life."[2]

Similarly, a famous quote attributed to philosopher Blaise Pascal helps us understand the unique longing that each person has that can only be fulfilled with the presence of God: "There is a God-shaped vacuum in the heart of each [human] which cannot be satisfied by any created thing but only by God

1. Augustine of Hippo, *The Confessions of St. Augustine: Modern English Version* (Revell, Baker Publishing Group, 2005), 15–16.

2. Thomas Merton, *Contemplative Prayer* (New York: Image Group, 2014), 5–6.

the Creator." But this is a mere paraphrase of Pascal's actual words, even if in principle they are similar enough to render a good interpretation of his thoughts: "What else does this craving, and this helplessness, proclaim but that there was once in [humanity] a true happiness, of which all that now remains is the empty print and trace? This he tries in vain to fill with everything around him, seeking in things that are not there the help he cannot find in those that are, though none can help, since this infinite abyss can be filled only with an infinite and immutable object; in other words by God himself."[3] As Pascal's words illustrate, only God can fill our deepest longings.

Henri Nouwen said it so well when he affirmed, "There is a deep hole in your being, like an abyss. You will never succeed in filling that hole because your needs are inexhaustible."[4] And until we are satisfied in God alone, our lives will remain in the void. David discovered this truth when he wrote, "My heart says of you, 'Seek his face!' Your face, LORD, I will seek" (Psalm 27:8). God rewards the quest to seek his face. Thus, our prayer is birthed in a deep desire to be immersed in his presence first as we enter his gates with thanksgiving in our hearts and adore his name.

---

3. Blaise Pascal, *Pensées* (New York: Penguin Classics, 2003), 75.
4. Henri J. M. Nouwen, *The Inner Voice of Love: A Journey through Anguish to Freedom* (New York: Image Books, 1999), 3.

Henri Nouwen is one of the greatest spiritual writers of modern times, and he once said, "Prayer is an attitude of an open heart, silently in tune with the Spirit of God, revealing itself in gratitude and contemplation."[5] Prayer, then, is not so much the memorization or recitation of a prescribed set of words or particular phrases that have been passed on through tradition and generations, although these certainly have their place in the practice of our Christian faith. But more fundamentally, prayer is the posture that a willing heart takes when humble, simple, and common words are directed to God in an attempt to express the condition of our soul. Whether these words come out of a state of desperation, desire, gratitude, or appreciation, prayer conveys the most profound and banal sentiments of our hearts. That is why prayer reveals in many ways one's highest aspirations and yearnings for *saturation* as well as one's deepest frustrations with *fragmentation* in our world. As we experience the detriments of a fallen world, coated with faded colors of brokenness and unreasonable loss, prayer becomes a mechanism by which these broken pieces can once again be put together and become saturated with hope, peace, and purpose. More than a tool, a weapon, or a strategy, prayer is a vehicle of love, a sign of hope, and a sigh of relief. For that reason, prayer is never superficial, even when it is simple. And

---

5. Nouwen, *Spiritual Direction: Wisdom for the Long Walk of Faith* (New York: HarperCollins, 2006), 62.

when words fail to adequately express our utter need for God and reliance on his supernatural intervention, prayer can transcend through groans, tears, silence, and exclamations.

In *Spiritual Direction*, Henri Nouwen recounts a parable told by renowned Russian author Leo Tolstoy that captures the essence of prayer:

> Three Russian monks lived on a faraway island. Nobody ever went there, but one day their bishop decided to make a pastoral visit. When he arrived, he discovered that the monks didn't even know the Lord's Prayer. So he spent all his time and energy teaching them the "Our Father" and then left, satisfied with his pastoral work. But when his ship had left the island and was back in the open sea, he suddenly noticed the three hermits walking on the water—in fact, they were running after the ship! When they reached it, they cried, "Dear Father, we have forgotten the prayer you taught us." The bishop, overwhelmed by what he was seeing and hearing, said, "But, dear brothers, how then do you pray?" They answered, "Well, we just say, "Dear God, there are three of us, and there are three of you: have mercy on us!" The bishop, awestruck by their sanctity and simplicity, said, "Go back to your land and be at peace."[6]

6. Nouwen, *Spiritual Direction*, 56.

Prayer is so simple yet so difficult for many of us. We think we have to have all the right words to communicate with our heavenly Father or be in the right mood to come close to his presence when, in reality, God is but a breath away. He waits for us to invite him to guide us, lead us, direct us, comfort us, move us, forgive us, and renew us. Sometimes when we don't know what to say or how to pray, one phrase will stop God in his tracks, as blind Bartimaeus found out: "Jesus, son of David, have mercy on me!" (Mark 10:47, 48). Even better, if you don't have much time to pray, or don't remember that Jesus is a descendant of King David, a simple prayer can have far-reaching effects: "Come near and rescue me" (Psalm 69:18). This rescue is what God's grace accomplishes for us as we invite him to come near, for if we shut him out of our lives he will not force his way in. His uncontrolling love always waits for us to open our hearts so that we may experience the redeeming power, restructuring mindset, restorative energy, and redefining moment that is possible when we freely choose to abandon ourselves to his grace.

Closing the Door to Noise

*But when you pray, go into your room, **close the door** and*
pray to your Father, who is unseen. Then your Father,
who sees what is done in secret, will reward you.
—*Matthew 6:6*

In order to open the door of dialogue with our heavenly
Father, we must first intentionally and purposefully close the
door to the noise that distracts us from nurturing a relationship with God. By closing the door to noise, I do not mean the
external noise that cannot be controlled, such as traffic noise,
neighborhood noise, or work noise—the many different types
of noise generated by full households, busy offices, hard-work-
ing factories, or active jobs that constantly demand our attention. In the modern world, unless we become hermits (living in
solitude), cenobites (living in intentional communities), or are
naturally contemplative like Mary, it will be difficult to *close
the door* completely or literally, although it is certainly important to establish for ourselves times of prayer that take us away
from the routine tasks of life. Instead, closing the door to noise
is an *internal* process that involves three steps.

First, we must close the door to the noise of worry. When
our thoughts are constantly anxiety-stricken, fear-filled, and
worry-plagued, we are unable to pray. But the moment we begin to lift up our eyes to the heavens and offer those concerns
wrapped up in the blankets of the unknown, we withdraw our

hearts from the tumultuous noise of the "what-ifs." As we silence our own thoughts and focus on his word, promise, and presence, prayer will become more engaging and dynamic.

Second, we must close the door to the noise of our daily responsibilities and activities that fill up every area of our minds. One of the things that hinders our prayers is the fact that we have not yet learned to center them on God or redirect them from a problem onto his promises. Instead we allow our minds to wander toward our feelings. We should not be annoyed with our mental wanderings but should simply refocus our attention, choosing to quiet the internal, incessant voice of activity while embracing a posture of internal poise.

Finally, we must close the door to the noise of selfish desires, which are so easily evoked through prayer. We must first recognize them and place them at the feet of the Father for him to purify them and, in the process, bring out the best in ourselves. When we surrender our wants and commit to God's will, prayer becomes more enjoyable and dynamic. After all, prayer is not about getting all of our wishes granted; it is about surrendering our will so that God's will may be done. This surrender can only happen when we trust that God sees what we cannot see and that his plan of redemption will ultimately prevail even if God answers a specific prayer with a no.

The Blessings of His Rewards

But when you pray, go into your room, close the door and
pray to your Father, who is unseen. Then your Father,
*who sees what is done in secret, **will reward you.***
—*Matthew 6:6*

The more we pray, the more we will discover that prayer is an invitation to a continuous conversation with almighty God. If we trust that God's will is perfect and pleasing and that God desires what is best for his children, then prayer will not be so focused on our needs and wants but on his presence and purpose. God sees every action under the heavens (Proverbs 15:3), weighs every motive of the heart (Proverbs 16:2), and perceives every thought from afar (Psalm 139:2). Before a word is on our tongue, God already knows it completely (Psalm 139:4). It would seem, then, somewhat foolish to think the purpose of prayer is to make God understand how we feel, to bargain with God, or to make him aware of our needs, for he *already knows.* Yet God *wants* us to tell him how we feel and what we desire and need because he cares about us and about every detail of our lives and wants us to communicate with him, like we would with a friend. He wants to be involved in our daily lives so we may learn to be guided by him. He cares about every aspect of our existence and desires a relationship with us, which means he also seeks connection and communication with his children because he loves us and desires to be one with us.

God does not always reward us in the way we think of rewards. When Matthew 6:6 says that God, who sees everything that is done in secret, will reward you, it means God will reward your pursuit of his presence; it does not necessarily refer to material rewards, although sometimes God's blessings come in practical, material, and physical ways so that we may become continual channels of God's grace. When thinking of material rewards, I am reminded of John, who was a lonely, wealthy, cantankerous old man. He worked hard all his life and built a great business that led to great financial success—but he was always alone. One Sunday evening as he was taking a walk around his neighborhood, he realized there was joyous music coming from an old church. John decided to slip into the service quietly so as to not be noticed, and he sat down in a pew in the back. At the close of the service the pastor asked if anyone present would like to give a testimony about how God had blessed them. After several people had spoken, John decided to stand up and share his story. He described how once, when he was a young boy, he had worked all day for a shiny silver dollar. At the end of the day, he was so proud of his accomplishment, and on his way home he heard music coming from a church just like this one. Drawn by the beautiful music, he went inside, and when it came time for the offering, the only money he had was the shiny silver dollar in his pocket. If he dropped the coin in the offering plate, he would be giving all he had, so it was a difficult decision. But when the offering plate got to him, he let go of that shiny coin and gave it away. He shared that that had been many years ago, but because he had not held anything back from God that night, God had truly blessed him in his life with great wealth. Full of pride, John sat back down. As he was taking his seat, a little old lady was overheard saying, "I dare you to do it again."

Here was John, thinking that God had rewarded him with great wealth because of a single moment of sacrificial giving when he was a young boy. In his mind, his great wealth and success were intricately connected to one event of surrender. But his thinking, though partly true, was inherently faulty. Undoubtedly, John had been blessed and had many reasons to be thankful. He rightly recognized that God was the source of his success, but John's ultimate conclusion was based on a simplistic understanding of causation. Causation is complex because a decision is always preceded by an antecedent, which in turn is influenced by a multiplicity of factors. To think there is an equation to get God to bless us or a magical formula that may entail a one-time gift or one-time prayer would be the same error as reducing God to a genie in a bottle. We do not give God X so he may give us back 10X, and neither do we just surrender our lives once and think that God will give us 10X because we gave X. The giving—the consecration, the surrender, the prayer—must be continual, ongoing, perpetual.

This is the mistake that most of us make in prayer. We think that God will reward our prayers with the answers we seek because, well, we prayed or because we prayed a lot! When we don't receive what we have prayed for, we either stop praying altogether, or we think we are not good enough or holy enough or deserving enough like others who did get what they prayed for. But that is not how God works. He does not sit on his glorious throne listening for compelling arguments as to why our wishes should be granted. God sees everything, and we do not. He knows everything, but we do not. This is where trust begins and reason ends. Will we trust that he knows what he is doing when prayer is not answered the way we expected? Will we trust that he has a plan to redeem our pain in the midst of brokenness and tragedy when the last thing we feel like doing is praying? Will we trust that prayer can accomplish much more than receiving answers in the way we think they should be given? There are only two possible answers to these questions. We can either say no and *resist,* or we can say yes and *release.* If we resist, the pain will be double in weight. For God desires to come near, but we turn away from the only true source of blessing who knows just what we need. If we release our fears, doubts, worry, and pain to him, prayer will naturally become a personalized exchange, in which the first blessing received will be the Spirit of God himself.

When teaching about prayer in the Sermon of the Mount, Jesus turned to his disciples and said, "Which of you, if your son asks for bread, will give him a stone? Or if he asks for a fish, will give him a snake? If you, then, though you are evil, know how to give good gifts to your children, how much more will your Father in heaven give good gifts to those who ask him!" (Matthew 7:9–11). Against a backdrop of increasingly faithful activity, we set our hearts on prayer, recognizing that the blessings of God's rewards come in many forms. In fact, answers to prayer are prone to appear wrapped up in a mantle of surprise, packaged in the smallest of boxes, and arriving at the most unpredictable times. Sometimes the blessings come in the form of God's tender solace. Other times, they appear in the form of a great miracle that no one can explain. Many times the answer is a new perspective. Sometimes the answer is still being forged as we wait silently, impatiently, or trembling in the fiery furnace. And sometimes the answer is no. Regardless of how God's good gifts come, the truth is that God always answers prayer and rewards what is done in the secret place.

Praying without Ceasing

*Rejoice always, **pray continually**, give thanks in all circumstances;*
for this is God's will for you in Christ Jesus.
—1 Thessalonians 5:16–18

Before delving into a discussion about what it means to pray without ceasing, let's first talk about what this phrase does not mean. Praying without ceasing does not mean we stop thinking or playing or working or resting because all we do is pray. To be in constant communion with God does not mean thinking about God to the exclusion of all other things, as if God should be separate from our daily lives. When we compartmentalize activities, separating them into sacred and secular, we allocate God to a transcendent realm and fail to see that God is also immanent—that is, here in the world, permanently pervading and sustaining the entire world. Since God is everywhere and can see everything, even the hidden motives of our hearts, dialoguing with God about how we truly feel is never a surprise to him. Thus, praying without ceasing entails shifting our perspective from ourselves onto God without disregarding ourselves. It involves nurturing the awareness of God's omniscience and omnipresence as well as recognizing and understanding our own strengths, weaknesses, and how we are individually wired. As we invite God into our lives and discuss with him our thoughts, feelings, concerns, and goals in life, he convicts, guides, leads, transforms, and helps us navigate the storms of life and enjoy the green pastures beside still waters.

In order to pray without ceasing, we must first nurture a suitable mindset. Prayer requires us to develop a mindset conducive to the practice of the presence of God—making room for God in our thoughts. We cannot pray without ceasing if we are consumed by our worries, selfish desires, and daily activities. But neither can we pray without ceasing if we are unable to invite God to be part of those thoughts and keep nothing hidden from him. We cannot pray without ceasing if we talk all the time and make no space to listen. But the moment we begin to shift our perspective and take our minds off all the jittery noise that weighs us down, we can invite God to help us sort through our intricate thoughts.

It would be almost impossible to empty our minds of all our concerns and problems because these constitute part of our human existence. In fact, in Scripture, we are never called to empty our minds—only our hearts. So it will require discipline on our part to train our thoughts. Our minds are the soil where both joy and sorrow, pain and desire meet. These are natural responses to the experiences of life. We can invite God into the inner chambers of our hearts and ask him to purify, bless, sanctify, or heal us in these areas. As Henri Nouwen has eloquently written, "To pray unceasingly is to channel our thoughts out of their fearful isolation into a fearless conversation with God."[7] By shifting our perspective from the problem onto God's presence, we can avoid spending too much time on introspection, lest we idolize the practice itself or become consumed by our own inadequacies instead of worshiping the God who reveals himself *during* introspection.

---

7. Nouwen, *Clowning in Rome: Reflections on Solitude, Celibacy, Prayer, and Contemplation* (New York: Image Books, 1979), 68.

This shift may at times be aided by focusing our attention on images that bring us closer to Christ. For example, in the little prayer chapel at the university where I work, there is a wall painted with several images that convey the suffering of Christ. On one side, there is a picture of a cup and on the other side a picture of fire. In the middle, the words "The Prayer of Faith" are written, and right above these words a dove is surrounded by light. By focusing my attention on this picture and these words, I am reminded that the prayer of faith invites us to embrace the cup of suffering as well as the hopeful, reviving fire of God as two sides of the same coin: faith. The prayer of faith is an invitation to embark on what has already been revealed and experienced by Christ.

Let me share the following illustration to demonstrate a key point when it comes to praying without ceasing. An optimistic farmer lived next to a cranky neighbor. As soon as the farmer woke up each day, he would say, "Good morning, God!"

Next to his farm lived a grouchy old woman whose morning greeting was more like, "Good grief! Morning?!"

The two could not be more opposite. Where he saw opportunity, she saw problems. Where he was content, she was distressed.

One morning the farmer exclaimed, "Look at that gorgeous sunrise!"

"Yeah," she countered, "It will probably get so hot the crops will scorch!"

During a spring shower, he would say, "Isn't this wonderful? The rain is giving the corn the drink it needs today!"

"And if it doesn't stop before too long," would come the sour answer, "we'll wish we'd taken out flood insurance!"

Convinced that he could instill a little sense of wonder in her attitude, he got a dog that could perform incredible tricks. One day he invited her to watch his dog do some of its tricks. "Fetch!" he exclaimed, as he tossed a stick out into the lake. The dog rushed after the stick, walked on the water, and retrieved it. "What do you think of that?" he asked, smiling.

"Not much of a dog," she remarked. "He can't even swim!"

When we pray, we can be like the farmer, or we can be like the woman. We can look at our circumstances and stress and complain, or we can look at God and recognize he is greater than any situation we may face here on earth and be thankful for one more day of life. When we expose our hearts, reveal our thoughts, and invite God to direct them and redirect us, we nurture a mindset of praying without ceasing. We begin to notice God at work in the everyday aspects of life. We grow to the point of sensing God's presence in the irreparable, in the weariness of a long night, and in the dead of winter. When we invite a loving God into a candid dialogue about every aspect of life, he is able to reproduce in us his very own life.

Persisting through Obstacles

Praying without ceasing also involves prayer that endures and perseveres, especially when strenuous situations attempt to extinguish our motivation, dampen our fervency, or stifle our faith. In the Sermon on the Mount, Jesus encourages his disciples with these words: "Ask and it will be given to you; seek and you will find; knock and the door will be opened to you. For everyone who asks receives; the one who seeks finds; and to the one who knocks, the door will be opened" (Matthew 7:7–8). The Greek verbs in verse 7 are imperative, implying a command, an exhortation. But in verse 8, the verbs become participles, implying continual action. This shift means that our asking should not be done only once but must be ongoing. Those who *keep* asking will receive, those who *keep* seeking will find, and those who *keep* knocking will have the door opened to them. Jesus encourages us to pray until we receive an answer, but the command is bracketed in an interesting paradox: we ought to pray as if the answer depends on our prayer while simultaneously trusting that everything already depends on God. We ask as if we do not know whether the door will be opened, but we keep on asking because we know the right one *will* be opened. Within this paradox, we find the best opportunity for perseverance.

When I was a college student, I ran track and cross country. After years of hard work, I qualified to run the marathon at the national competition during my senior year. In preparation for the race of my life, I trained long hours every day. When the big day finally came, I was ready. The race started slow. After all, we had twenty-six miles in front of us. By mile fifteen, I found myself in second place. For the next five miles, I competed next to another girl who was not going to let me win easily. By mile nineteen, I thought, *I need to get rid of this girl,* so I sped up a little, but so did she. At mile twenty-one, I hit the famous "runner's wall." If you are a runner, you know what I'm talking about. It's not the greatest feeling. It does not matter what you tell your body—it will not respond to your commands. At mile twenty-two, runners were starting to pass me, and by mile twenty-three I could barely move. I had side stitches, my legs were cramping, and I thought about quitting.

But I heard the voice of my coach along the road: "Keep going, don't give up now, you are almost there!"

So I approached mile twenty-four no longer thinking about quitting. Instead, I was thinking about dying. It seemed much more likely and appealing at the time! But I had only two miles left, so I pushed myself little by little until I saw the finish line, and as soon as I crossed it, I collapsed and passed out. I was so dehydrated I became delirious. My coach thought I was speaking Spanish, but God knows it was actually some sort of angelic tongue preparing me for my eternal home! I did not win that day. But I finished the race, and I can say I ran a marathon.

And so it is with prayer. Sometimes we will feel the rhythms of joy so deeply etched in our memories or hear the beautiful sound of otherworldly music so vividly imprinted in our hearts as we recall or experience a meaningful time of glory. In those times, it will become almost inevitable to want to join a choir of angels. But there will be other times when the deep silence of God, the dark night of the soul, unmet expectations, the disillusion of a prayer that feels unanswered, or the simple interference of fear, doubt, anxiety, and defeat will place great hurdles along our paths for us to overcome. The best way to overcome them is through unceasing prayer, prayer that brings both the beautiful and the ugly, the sorrowful and the joyful, the pleasing and the shameful aspects of life together and offers all of it to the God who sees, receives, responds, and is able to heal and transform. And, as we persist through the many obstacles that will attempt to make us quit the race of faith, we might hear the voice of God along the way: *Keep going, don't give up now, you are almost there!*

2 ✳ MEDITATING ON THE CHARACTER OF GOD

I still remember my first date with my husband, Andrew. After much deliberation as to where we should go that evening, I suggested driving to Chicago, which was fifty miles away from where we lived. With a certain degree of surprise and reluctance, Andrew agreed, and we drove to the city to walk downtown in the cool of the evening. I could not believe I would get to sit next to the man of my dreams for the next hour, asking questions about his life, his interests, and his past—and he would do the same with me. Andrew was brilliant, well known, attractive, strong, determined, respected, compassionate, and funny. But he was American, and I was Brazilian, and we saw the world very differently. I knew it would take a lot of work to reconcile some of our differences. But, the more I got to know him, the more I trusted him with my heart. And the rest is history!

As we approach God through prayer, the first building block in establishing a connection that will enable us to trust him with our hearts is to know who he is and what he is like. How can we pray and connect with someone we don't know? Admittedly, trying to comprehend God is like hiking a mountain that has an unreachable peak, or diving into an ocean whose depths we can never reach, or trying to grasp the wind that always escapes us. Trying to understand God in all of his existence is beyond us. Nevertheless, we can know *some things* about God as revealed through Scripture. Knowing his character can help us connect with his heart and purposes as we dialogue with him. It would be beyond the scope of this chapter to describe all the attributes of God and list all his characteristics, but I have chosen five qualities that represent the core of his nature so that, as we pray in light of our own circumstances and human realities, we may pray boldly and confidently, recognizing who he is. After all, God sees life very differently than we do, and it takes a lifetime of obedience to reconcile our differences. But prayer makes this possible.

1. The Holiness of God in Light of Our Sinfulness

The willful act in the garden of Eden to fail to submit to the will of God brought about an internal break to our human experience, infecting our nature with a sinful condition and our environment with a sullied disorder. Despite the fact that humanity was made in the image and likeness of God, every inclination of the thoughts of the human heart became evil (Genesis 6:5; 8:21). Although the image of God has remained imprinted in us, evidenced by our worth to God, the likeness of God in us was polluted and eroded, making us unworthy of God.

Isaiah realized his unworthiness the moment he saw the glory of God: "'Woe to me!' I cried. 'I am ruined! For I am a man of unclean lips, and I live among a people of unclean lips, and my eyes have seen the King, the LORD Almighty'" (6:5).

Job, despite all his suffering and the pain that once blocked his vision of God, came to that same place of awareness: "My ears had heard of you but now my eyes have seen you. Therefore I despise myself and repent in dust and ashes" (42:5–6).

The apostle Paul recognized his unworthiness and said, "What a wretched man I am! Who will rescue me from this body that is subject to death?" (Romans 7:24).

Until we see ourselves the way God sees us, prayer will remain *transactional* instead of *transformational*. And until we see God as he is, prayer will only be a *preoccupation* with our needs instead of becoming a *pursuit* of God's will.

Everything about God is holy. His Word is holy. His Spirit is holy. His nature is holy. Naturally, God's primary concern is with the holiness, wholeness, and health of his creation. But for his creation to come alive and become whole again, God must destroy whatever destroys creation's wholeness and health. As such, the holiness of God, his love for creation, and his wrath toward sin are intricately interwoven and inseparable. God's wrath is shown through his unquenchable zeal for justice and righteousness. God's love is displayed through his self-giving and sacrificial gift to rescue and redeem what is broken and lost. His love and wrath, as well as his glory and righteousness, conform his holiness. And his holiness sets him apart.

We are called to be holy: "For it is written: 'Be holy, because I am holy'" (1 Peter 1:16). Of course, this New Testament scripture is quoting and repeating the same instruction from the Old Testament, found in Leviticus 11:44, 45, and 19:2. This call for humanity to share in God's holiness is only made possible because of the sacrifice of Jesus Christ. The call is not to be holy *in the same way* that God is holy, for that would demand something we could never fulfill or attain. It is simply a call to come to God and allow him to purify our unrighteousness and make us righteous (holy) in him. It is a command to desire God above anything else. Holiness is made possible by descending into the valley of self-surrender and climbing the rocky slopes toward refinement. As we recognize our state of brokenness and sinfulness that deprives us of God's holiness, we repent and turn away from what is ultimately destroying us. As we behold the beauty of the King and approach him in his majesty, we cannot help but adore him for what he is remaking

in us. Even when the process might be painful, we know the outcome will be worth it in the end.

When we love God for who he is, our prayer is centered on his holy presence. Prayer then allows us to participate in the worshipful cantata that goes on day and night in the heavenly realm: "Holy, holy, holy is the Lord God Almighty, who was, and is, and is to come" (Revelation 4:8). We may fall down before him like the elders at the sight of his majestic glory, worshiping him for all that he is and has done: "You are worthy, our Lord and God, to receive glory and honor and power, for you created all things, and by your will they were created and have their being" (v. 11). However, the external position we take when we pray is secondary to our internal posture. God desires to make us one with him. The first step is to recognize our dire need to be like him, which can only come as we admit that his love for us is extended as a sign of acceptance of who we are, with all our flaws and imperfections. He consistently calls us to more than we presently are. Prayer invites us to respond to the call to be like him in his love and holiness every single day.

Who among the gods is like you, LORD? Who is like you—
majestic in holiness, awesome in glory, working wonders?
Exodus 15:11

41

Ascribe to the LORD, you heavenly beings, ascribe to the LORD
glory and strength. Ascribe to the LORD the glory due his name;
worship the LORD in the splendor of his holiness.
Psalm 29:1–2

Worship the LORD in the splendor of his holiness;
tremble before him, all the earth.
Psalm 96:9

2. The Goodness of God in Light of Our Tragedies

To set the tone for a brief discussion on the goodness of God, I will start with a short tale about the way tragedy tends to affect our perspective of what is good and noble. A Chinese farmer had a horse that was valuable to him. One day his only horse ran away. Upon hearing the predicament, some of his neighbors came over and said, "We're so sorry about your horse! The only one you had! What a tragedy!"

But the farmer said, "I don't know if it's good or bad—we'll see."

Two days later, as the neighbors were watering the crops, they saw the old horse return with twelve younger, healthier horses following him. The neighbors came over again and said to the farmer, "Oh, how fortunate you are! You must be very happy!"

And the farmer said, "Maybe. We will see."

The next morning, the farmer's only son went out to train the wild horses, but he was thrown to the ground and broke his leg. Several of the neighbors came over and said, "Oh, what a tragedy! Now you will have to farm all by yourself!"

"Who knows if it's good or bad?" said the farmer.

Several days later a war broke out, and all the young men were summoned to fight, except for the farmer's son, whose leg was broken. All the neighbors came over and said, "Oh, how fortunate you are! All our sons are gone to fight except yours, whom you still have here by your side."

Many are the interpretations of this story. A popular one is that no event in life is, in and of itself, good or bad; we decide what meaning to ascribe to each event. Therefore, we can be like the neighbors, quick to judge life's occurrences and label them as unfortunate or fortunate, or we can be like the farmer, who sees each event as one link connected to a larger set of links that make up a chain. But this rendering of the story's meaning is inadequate because, if we act like the neighbors, our perception of life will be largely influenced by the meaning we attach to the events themselves, limiting our perspective and hindering us from seeing a larger picture that may develop from the event itself. But if we are like the farmer, we might succumb to an escapist mentality, detaching ourselves from feeling pain or pleasure too closely, lest they become our sole reality or fearing we might become prey to masochistic or hedonistic mindsets.

There is a better way to understand the wisdom in this story by intertwining both attitudes together and allowing ourselves to feel the pain of tragedy or endure difficulties that beset us while *at the same time* recognizing that the present challenge is part of a greater story that God is weaving from which beautiful possibilities can emerge despite and beyond our present circumstances. It would be imprudent to conclude that unfortunate and tragic occurrences are "blessings in disguise" or that God ordains these kinds of events to refine our faith, even if in the end they end up having such effect. The reality of pain and suffering should not be denied or minimized. It should be felt, released, and offered to God. It would be foolish to hide our pain, suffering, and mourning. Embracing pain is a necessary step in the process toward healing and enjoying the beauty of life and the goodness of God.

I have seen and experienced hardship in ways that cannot be fully described or understood, and I have made the mistake of identifying with my suffering too closely and with the pain of others too deeply, making me prone to the error of thinking and seeing only gloom without being able to enjoy the radiance of the sunlight on a chilly day. In all our suffering and pain, there is another side less spoken about that often meanders on the path of irony; if we are not careful, we might miss it if we walk too fast. Joy, love, hope, and faith are ever-present companions. Even though the Bible identifies them as the fruit of the Spirit, they are also marks of God's goodness and grace, which he readily imprints upon souls longing to be lavished with his grace. He does not do so with the intention of preventing suffering or mitigating grief or numbing agony. He does not give them as tokens for enduring whatever affliction has befallen us. Some life occurrences cannot be fully eroded from the soil of our memory. They are to be accepted as part of our present human condition and a reminder of our frail humanity. This acceptance enables us to surrender it and offer it to him, who alone can redeem our pain, bring healing to our wounds, conquer our fears, and use our suffering to grow us and mature us, making us more resilient, patient, and kind along the way.

When we suffer or go through tragedy, we may be tempted to filter the character of God and our own worth through our earthly experiences, thereby concluding that either God is not good, or we are not good *enough*. This filtered perception colors our self-existence, and the way we view God becomes clouded by this faulty observation. Surely, what snuffs out prayer is the memory of false hope. Yet prayer is always an act of trust. Even when false hopes, painful realities, and irreparable loss might obliterate the foundation of our faith, the character of God remains intact, as observed in the person of Christ. C. S. Lewis came to this realization in *A Grief Observed*, writing, "What reason have we, except our own desperate wishes, to believe that God is, by any standard we can conceive, 'good'? Doesn't all the *prima facie* evidence suggest exactly the opposite? What have we to set against it? We set Christ against it."[1]

Truthfully, God cannot contradict his own nature. He is either good, or he is not. And if God is good, then tragedy and suffering are neither caused by him nor sent directly from him. God may allow the natural consequences of human behavior and free will to occur without interference—these realities occur as a result of living in a broken and sinful world. But God weeps with us, suffers with us, and prays for us. That's why, when we pray, we must meditate on the goodness of God and bring back to our memory all the ways in which he has been faithful in the past and all the ways we trust him to bring restoration in the future. The goodness of God is self-originated, inherent, eternal, and perfect.

A. W. Tozer, in *The Knowledge of the Holy*, affirms that God "has never been kinder than he is now, nor will he ever be less kind."[2] God sends the rain on the righteous and the unrighteous and makes the sun shine equally on both. God's goodness is like a fountain of living water in the desert. Even in

---

1. C. S. Lewis, *A Grief Observed* (New York: HarperOne, 1996), 29.
2. A. W. Tozer, *The Knowledge of the Holy*, (Digital Fire, Kindle Edition, 2019), 106.

times of deep loss and drought, hope, joy, wholeness, and favor can resurface and materialize little by little. When prayer places its mark of confidence in the goodness of God, we are able to enjoy what is truly good and allow his gifts of restoration to be unleashed one breath at a time, one tear after another.

Surely your goodness and love will follow me all the days of my life, and I will dwell in the house of the Lord *forever.*
Psalm 23:6

I remain confident of this: I will see the goodness of the Lord *in the land of the living.*
Psalm 27:13

Taste and see that the Lord *is good; blessed is the one who takes refuge in him.*
Psalm 34:8

Every good and perfect gift is from above, coming down from the Father of the heavenly lights, who does not change like shifting shadows.
James 1:17

3. The Love of God in Light of Our Rejections

Prayer is a gift, but we often neglect it or put it aside amidst life's many demands. Intuitively, prayer requires little effort when food is on the table or when we lie down to sleep. We readily recognize that God is our faithful provider whose unfailing love and everlasting mercy never end. But in moments when we seem unable to turn to God because our hearts are fragile, having become the target of criticism, accusations, judgment, abuse, or attacks, our view of God's love might become blurred. Consequently, we might cease to pursue him with all of our hearts, or become too busy with our daily lives, seeking to cover up the pain we feel inside with the many activities that have filled our schedules. But the truth is that his love is relentless, and he never stops pursuing us. In fact, his self-giving love becomes the most compelling force in the universe—drawing us, summoning us, calling us, and beckoning us at every point to be freed from whatever has imprisoned us. His love is perfect, profound, and eternal. A. W. Tozer remarks, "Because God is self-existent, his love had no beginning; because he is eternal, his love can have no end; because he is infinite, it has no limit; because he is holy, it is the quintessence of all spotless purity; because he is immense, his love is an incomprehensively vast, bottomless, shoreless sea."[3]

Many situations could potentially hinder us from understanding the power of God's love: a distant family, a broken marriage, a stern parent, a terminal illness, an abusive relationship, a seemingly irreparable mistake—and the list goes on. But the moment we decide to approach God empty-handed,

---

3. Tozer, *Knowledge of the Holy*, 128.

naked, vulnerable, without much to give, prove, or show, his all-consuming, never-failing, heart-wrenching love will at once clothe us with his acceptance and liberate us from the chains of insufficiency. The moment we approach God in the position of a child and allow him to embrace us with his tenderness, we embark on a life-giving and self-abandoning journey. As we focus on the extent of God's love for us, we will be enabled to walk in the power and freedom of our truest selves. Thomas Merton reminds us, "We are most truly ourselves when we lose ourselves. We become ourselves when we find ourselves in Christ."[4] And this can only happen through the vulnerability and honesty of prayer.

Even when we reject God, God pursues us. Even when we cannot find or feel God, he is always present. And even in the midst of our worst possible life rejections, God is forever faithful. This type of conviction, deeply rooted in the love of God, led the apostle Paul to say, "For I am convinced that neither death nor life, neither angels nor demons, neither the present nor the future, nor any powers, neither height nor depth, nor anything else in all creation, will be able to separate us from the love of God that is in Christ Jesus our Lord" (Romans 8:38–39). In this fertile ground of assurance, prayer will allow

---

4. Quoted in Susan Muto, "Living Contemplatively and Serving God in the World: Two Sides of the Coin in Christian Ministry," *Journal of Spiritual Formation & Soul Care*, Vol. 6 No. 1 (2013): 82.

us to experience what only God can give us: love that is both unconditional and uncontrolling.

> *How priceless is your unfailing love, O God!*
> *People take refuge in the shadow of your wings.*
> Psalm 36:7

> *Rise up and help us; rescue us because of your unfailing love.*
> Psalm 44:26

> *And hope does not put us to shame, because God's love*
> *has been poured out into our hearts through the Holy Spirit,*
> *who has been given to us.*
> Romans 5:5

4. The Grace of God in Light of Our Despair

There is perhaps no better way to understand the unique gift of prayer than when we turn our attention to the reality of God's grace. Grace is the hallmark of God's greatness and the epitome of his majesty. Grace is the most undeserving, unshakable, and unmerited gift one could ever receive. And this gift is simply a prayer away. Because grace is free, we often take it for granted. But because it is costly, we do not always pursue it. Grace is not a quick shower after playing in the mud of contempt; it is a full-blown immersion in the rivers of mercy, where the streams never stop flowing with gratitude along the banks. Grace is both a deliberate dive into the sea of repentance and a swift landing onto the tracks of forgiveness. Simply said, grace is God's favor gently bestowed upon a forlorn, desperate soul seeking to be consoled.

To help us understand how grace works, Jesus tells the parable of a Pharisee who is obsessed with his own virtues and a tax collector who recognizes his own state of misery. The Pharisee stood by himself and thanked God that he was not like others, for he tithed and fasted twice a week. The Pharisee was concerned with making himself superior because of his religious piety. The tax collector stood at a distance and would not even dare look up to heaven, beating his chest and crying out, "God, have mercy on me, a sinner" (Luke 18:13). It is interesting that Jesus would choose a Pharisee and a tax collector to show us whom we ought to emulate. His Jewish listeners would probably rather be like the Pharisee, who seemingly did everything right and was socially respected for his morality and punctilious religiosity instead of the tax collector, who was disliked for collaborating with the Roman Empire and often employed treacherous methods of taxation to advance his own position in society. But their vocations and positions of prestige are not what Jesus is concerned with. Instead, it is the candid realization that humility is the pathway to the gates of grace and that, without grace, we cannot move forward in our spiritual evolution. Jesus is saying we ought to be like those who recognize their unworthiness before God and confess their need for more of him, regardless of how far we have gone or what we have done—for grace always brings us back to the path of freedom.

The gift of grace is readily available for every single person who desires to possess it. Grace comes in many forms. *Prevenient grace* comes knocking at our door even before we are aware we need to let it in. *Saving grace* is presented when we are reconciled to God by faith through the sacrifice of Christ. *Sanctifying grace* is at work from the moment we receive saving grace, calling us deeper into God's life so we may experience the presence, power, and purity of his Spirit. *Healing grace* is offered when life's deep hurts pile up and our many wounds corrode our sense of worth.

Grace must be continually sought and received. The moment we stop seeking it, we return to our self-righteous position, thinking that somehow we have obtained enough to satisfy our needs or enough to make us feel better than those who haven't obtained it. The moment we fail to seek mercy and grace, we succumb to the very reality we have been trying to escape, making us kingly prigs or pretentious queens all over again. Without daring to continually seek grace, we become our most dreaded masters and our worst, most implacable foes. If we recognize that grace is the remedy to our condition, we will never cease to take it. For it is only God's unmerited, unlimited, unbreakable grace that can sustain us. A contrite heart and lowly spirit create good space in our beings to receive this grace. The grace of God not only invites us to accept our limitations and forgive our past mistakes but also compels us to extend grace to others when they wrong or hurt us.

For it is by grace you have been saved, through faith—
and this is not from yourselves, it is the gift of God—
not by works, so that no one can boast.
Ephesians 2:8–9

Let us then approach God's throne of grace with confidence,
so that we may receive mercy and find grace to help us
in our time of need.
Hebrews 4:16

But he gives us more grace. That is why Scripture says:
"God opposes the proud but shows favor to the humble."
James 4:6

5. The Omnipotence of God in Light of Our Impotence

We often hear that there is nothing impossible for God. And, in a sense, this is true because God is omnipotent, which means he is capable of creating and doing anything. But omnipotence also means that God has the ability to choose to limit God's own power by establishing certain laws that can be called universal, or natural. Omnipotence also means that God may choose when or when not to transgress these laws.

One of those laws is the law of free will. God's love allows humanity the freedom of personal choice. He made humanity with the capacity to choose between right and wrong, between humanity's desires and God's desires. But the moment we empty ourselves, become surrendered vessels, and deconstruct our negligent patterns of thinking, numerous possibilities open up, allowing God to be able to work in unprecedented ways. Our human impossibilities, dire circumstances, and difficult situations become opportunities for his power, strength, supremacy, and authority to be revealed.

Let us consider an interesting scenario that Jesus presented to his disciples after his teaching on how we should pray. In Luke, the Lord's Prayer is shorter than the version we have learned to recite from the Matthew account, and is followed by this illustration:

Then Jesus said to them, "Suppose you have a friend, and you go to him at midnight and say, 'Friend, lend me three loaves of bread; a friend of mine on a journey has come to me, and I have no food to offer him.' And suppose the one inside answers, 'Don't bother me. The door is already locked, and my children and I are in bed. I can't get up and give you anything.' I tell you, even though he will not get up and give you the bread because of friendship, yet because of your shameless audacity he will surely get up and give you as much as you need." (Luke 11:5–8)

In this account, Jesus is showing us a few things about our human deprivations and our Father's bounty. A man on a journey shows up at a friend's door and needs some basic hospitality—food and shelter. His friend has no sustenance in that moment to offer him, but he does know of another friend who might be able to help, which is what drives him to visit his other friend at midnight in hopes of obtaining some food. The people of God in this world are like the friend who doesn't have his own resources to offer but knows where to get them. Our Father is like the friend who has enough bread. God has all the resources we need. Partnering with God is a matter of figuring out how to get God's resources to those who need them. God is not a stingy God who wants to keep all his power to himself. Sometimes he can't find vessels that are emptied enough of their own control to be adequate carriers of his power and through whom he may work. That is one reason we may feel like we don't see his power displayed frequently enough. At other times, God may choose not to intervene because his plans and purposes are far beyond our comprehension, and we must trust that his ways and thoughts are higher than ours.

Interestingly enough, Jesus does not focus in this story on the friend not giving the man what he wanted. If we are careful, we may notice that the persistence and boldness of the man's request gets the attention of the friend inside the house. He came at the most inopportune time—at midnight—and asked for help. What Jesus is saying in this teaching on prayer is that prayer opens the way for God to provide, to work in and through us, and to satisfy every need we may have, no matter how big or small. God sees our pain. He sees our loneliness. He hears our prayers. It may be midnight or midday, but he always fulfills what he promises, for he is faithful.

Prayer connects us to those innumerable possibilities and opportunities that are found in God and makes them accessible to us. We should not stop asking if the door gets slammed in our face. Mustering up enough courage, humility, and boldness, we should knock again and again, recognizing that God has what we need and will give us what we need (which, we should remember, is not always exactly what we ask for) in the proper time and way. Andrew Murray, missionary and prolific writer, once said, "In prayer we secure the presence and power of God. . . . Between our impotence and God's omnipotence, intercession is the blessed link."[5]

I know that you can do all things;
no purpose of yours can be thwarted.
Job 42:2

---

5. Andrew Murray, *The Ministry of Intercession: A Plea for More Prayer* (Springdale, PA: Whitaker House, 1982), 38.

Great is our Lord and mighty in power;
his understanding has no limit.
Psalm 147:5

See, I am the LORD, *the God of all flesh;*
is anything too hard for me?
Jeremiah 32:27 (NRSVUE)

But Jesus looked at them and said, "With man this is impossible,
but with God all things are possible."
Matthew 19:26

3 ❋ UNITING OUR HEARTS WITH THE PURPOSES OF GOD

If the primary goal of prayer is to connect with the heart of God, then God's goal is for us to hear his heartbeat for the world so we may partner with God in his mission of rescue and redemption. God invites us to know him so we may know what is in God's heart. Julian of Norwich, a medieval contemplative, once said, "The whole reason we pray is to be united into the vision and contemplation of him to whom we pray."[1] God's ultimate desire is to bring us into a place of surrender so we may experience his power, presence, purity, and holiness. Prayer serves to oil our wheels, empowering us from the inside to live out the Christian life with vitality as we are energized by the life-giving Spirit.

1. Julian of Norwich, *Showings* (Mahwah, New Jersey: Paulist Press, 1978), 254.

Structural Prayer

When we become Christians, we are said to be "united with Christ," which means we are like branches grafted onto a vine so the life of Christ may be infused into us. One of the ways this happens is through what I call "structural prayer." Structural prayer begins with the acknowledgment that something inside us needs to be formed if we are to grow in Christ. God desires to restore what is damaged inside us, bringing us into a state of oneness with him so we may hear his heartbeat for the world and become co-participants in his mission of rescue. In our daily, mundane concerns and the familiarity of brokenness, loss, and pain, God desires to reveal the areas in our lives that have been marred by difficult experiences and created holes in our souls. God desires to realign us with himself, but we must first recognize, expose, and deal with the holes in our lives so God might fill them and restore them with his all-consuming love.

Life brings painful and hurtful experiences that, if left unaddressed, will create fractures in our souls that may lead to the formation of boulders of dysfunction that are intended to mitigate, cover up, minimize, or escape the pain we feel inside. They might be boulders of addiction, of perfectionism, of criticism, of consumerism, of pessimism, of ambition, or something else. These boulders are safeguarded by layers of fear, anger, grief, pride, and more.

Imagine you purchased a pair of gloves that, much like a pair of new shoes, came with wrinkled paper inside. Now let's pretend that we are the glove, made in the exact image of the hand, which is God. The hand desires to fill the glove, but it cannot fill it to the fullest until the wrinkled debris of the paper is removed. Recognizing the layers of accumulated debris inside ourselves is the first step toward allowing the Spirit of God to enliven us, which can only happen if we invite God into those spaces through honest, confessional, repentant prayer. Because only the Spirit of God convicts, asking God to reveal the areas in our lives that need his touch and repair becomes necessary. Prayer of contemplation requires us to take a deep look at our broken selves and recognize that, if we are to be like him, we must first be *with* him, talk with him, and bring to him those things that are blocking his way so we may unite our hearts with his and step into our destiny with freedom and purpose through structural prayer.

Jesus was adamant that if we are to follow him we must deny ourselves (Matthew 16:24). Denying ourselves does not mean rejecting our personhood. On the contrary, it means we bring our personhood to its fullest capacity by affirming what is intrinsically good in us, controlling what has the potential to lead us astray, and rejecting what has been marred by sinful tendencies, generational patterns, and personal choices that are not in alignment with God's character or his desires for us.

One way we can seek resolution for our internal conflicts is through prayer for inner healing. Theologians and practitioners such as David Seamands and Terry Wardle, who are both seminary professors and avid writers on the topic, shed light on the value of this approach from a pastoral perspective. In *Healing for Damaged Emotions*, for example, Seamands provides a careful explanation of how God desires to bring healing to damaged emotions and encounters individuals in places of past hurt in order to bring healing to our memories. Likewise, Terry Wardle's extensive work on healing prayer lays out an important foundation to help the broken find wholeness in Christ. His approach is based on years of careful research as well as his own personal experience with what he calls *formational prayer*. Wardle's general style aligns with a pastoral counseling approach, highlighting in particular the role of prayer and the work of the Holy Spirit, who is able to bring healing to the emotional and mental capacities of our broken human lives.

Prayer for Inner Healing

Our souls become fractured when we experience traumatic events or severe wounding. If these wounds are not properly healed by God's grace, they become fertile ground for the formation of false beliefs and distorted views about ourselves, God, and others. This distorted view of reality leads to a natural emotional upheaval, and anxiety, depression, and overwhelming grief are only a few of the uninvited symptoms we will experience, which may in turn lead to a variety of dysfunctional behaviors to numb the pain we feel inside. These wounds of the past can leak into the present and distort the way we view God, people, and ourselves, limiting our ability to love well while potentially leading to the formation of strongholds of fear, shame, guilt, bitterness, and control. If we are to love like Jesus and live like Jesus, we need the grace of Jesus to help us get unstuck in the various places where we have been wounded.

Imagine for a moment that, when you were a child, your mother repeatedly criticized you for not doing things right, which led to a wound in your soul. Mothers are supposed to provide safe and caring environments, but probably because your mother was wounded herself and did not recognize it, you became the target of her hurt. Every time you did not do something exactly as she wanted, she made the same comment: "Not like that! This is the way you do it!" Her words hurt and embarrassed you, especially when they were spoken in front of the whole family because it caused you to feel insecure.

Over time, those words sank so deeply into your subconscious mind that you began to believe what your mom said. You began to think, *I can never do anything right!* and, *I'm not good enough.* These false beliefs about yourself caused a distorted view of the world to take shape. Living with those false beliefs became difficult because you tried to compensate in

63

other ways. You might have felt sad, embarrassed, depressed, or ashamed, or you might have reacted in more aggressive ways depending on your personality. In order to numb the pain, you coped with food addiction. As an adult, you now are dealing with some health issues, but no one has considered that there might be a link between your current health and your mother's hurtful words that created a deep wound in your soul. People look at you and think you are normal, but deep inside there is a distortion of reality that is causing you real problems.

So what's the answer? There is certainly not a magic pill or a one-time fix. There is a process of restoration and a journey toward healing that must take place. The first step in that process is for us to invite Jesus into our places of deep wounding so we can experience his amazing grace and comfort. Our negative memories can be touched by his healing grace and transformed into life-giving opportunities of love, forgiveness, confidence, and purpose. This transformation happens progressively as we seek to merge the broken pieces of ourselves into our *true* selves. Henri Nouwen said it like this: "You have to move gradually from crying outward—crying out for people whom you think can fulfill your needs—to crying inward to the place where you can let yourself be held and carried by God, who has become incarnate in the humanity of those who love you in community."[2]

---

2. Nouwen, *The Inner Voice of Love*, 7.

The prayer for inner healing positions us before Jesus to bring deep-level healing to our wounds so we can be formed into the image of Jesus and find our true identity in Christ. Validating our feelings is important in the process because emotions are indicators of what is causing us pain.

The journey toward healing happens through a process, with the help of the Holy Spirit and the support and care of other Christians. In some cases, where strongholds may have developed over time, deliverance prayers and professional counseling may be necessary. It would be beyond the scope of this book to discuss the myriad ways the prayer for inner healing may be useful and helpful to move forward spiritually, but several ministries have been developed specifically to help individuals find emotional healing.

The reality is that individuals dealing with emotional instability or mental health issues may require more than a prayer for inner healing to process life. Prayer will only open the door for releasing and confessing what needs to be addressed. It would be misleading and simplistic to assume that all our issues could be resolved through prayer. Any combination of factors can contribute to our internal mayhem, including but not limited to family of origin issues, biomedical factors, psychological disorders, relational tension, lifestyle issues, life stressors, unconfessed sin, and spiritual warfare. Therefore, it is always important to consider a combination of factors as contributing to the upheaval in someone's life and not just one factor. As such, it becomes imperative to be more integrative, careful, and holistic in our approaches to bring healing to the emotional side, taking into consideration the interrelationships among the spiritual, personal, cultural, social, and psychological aspects of our human existence.

The process toward restoration and healing may be arduous because we live in a broken world with broken systems that constantly affect us. Here, however, I want to suggest a few ways by which we can release and relinquish our self-protective layers that may hinder us from coming into union with God's purposes so that, as we offer them to God, a true exchange may be produced.

Overcoming Fear

To a certain degree, fear is normal. Fear is something we all experience, and we cannot easily deny or escape it. Fear usually likes to hang out with its cousins, anxiety and worry, threatening to disturb the quiet corners of our minds. Fear is a terrible companion. It keeps us up late at night and busy during the day. Fear knocks uninvited on our door at the most inopportune times, constantly changing the direction of our own mental conversations. We might fear losing someone or something important to us. We might fear the unknown, or we may fear being alone. We may fear what others might think about us or do to us. Many are the fears that, like any uninvited guest, might try to run full speed and force their way into a weary mind or fractured heart to settle there until told they are no longer welcome. Having the courage to face our fears is the first step toward resisting their debilitating grip. Having courage does not mean we will not be afraid. It simply means we will not let fear stop us from moving forward and pursuing what lies ahead.

I am reminded of Johnny, a five-year-old boy, who happened to be in the kitchen when his mother was making supper. She asked him to go into the pantry and get her a can of tomato soup, but he refused to go in alone.

"It's dark in there, and I'm scared," he said.

She asked again, but he was too afraid to go in by himself. Finally, she said, "It's okay, Johnny. Jesus will be in there with you."

Johnny hesitated but then decided to walk to the pantry and slowly open the door. He peeked inside, saw it was dark, and started to close the door. The mother heard him say as he sheepishly looked away, "Jesus, if you're in there, can you hand me that can of tomato soup?"

Just like Johnny did, sometimes the best way to overcome fear is to take a step *toward* what makes us afraid. David was right when he said, "When I am afraid, I put my trust in you. In God, whose word I praise—in God I trust and am not afraid. What can mere mortals do to me?" (Psalm 56:3–4). David recognized that sometimes fear will assault us. It might grip us, and it might try to shackle us, but the type of fear that paralyzes us with daunting dread should alert us that it is working against us to try to keep us from stepping into our calling or pursuing God's heart for the world. This type of paralyzing fear should be defeated by taking a simple step toward what we fear most. The moment we take the first step, we recognize that fear was ruthlessly trying to keep us away from allowing our truest selves to emerge.

A practical way to defeat fear is to step into the object of your fear and recognize that fear was the obstacle all along. Then ask yourself, *What am I afraid of losing? What am I afraid of doing?* By surrendering the object of your fear, you recognize that fear was hindering you from taking a step of trust in your relationship with the Lord and that, through surrender, fear loses its grip and power over you.

Fear can be a powerful motivator. If we fear losing something important, we will work harder to keep it—but those who trust in God can learn a different response to fear. If we subscribe to a mentality of danger and worry, fear can make us flee from new opportunities. On the other hand, if we walk with God, our fear can propel us to face uncertain situations with courage and trust, recognizing that if we don't try we will never know what we might gain. The choice is always personal—but if you choose to step outside of fear, you might discover that perhaps the greatest enemy holding you back from taking what is yours by faith has been fear itself.

Releasing Anger

Anger is a natural response to life's unfair situations, hurts, and pain. God got angry at the Israelites. Jesus got angry in the temple. Paul got angry with Peter. We should expect that anger is a normal experience of life. But the Bible encourages us not to sin in our anger (Ephesians 4:26).

Humans have a natural tendency to feel offended when we are angry. We may then harbor resentment or desire revenge. We may operate like shields, trying to keep everyone and everything away in an effort to protect ourselves. Or we may act like swords, accusing, criticizing, and pointing the finger at what others are doing wrong. Both shielding ourselves and striking out are destructive and unproductive tendencies.

Anger comes in many shapes and forms. There is *blazing* anger, where we may show our frustration through fits of rage. There is also *brooding* anger, when we become bitter and resentful, two poisonous emotions that will erode the soil of our hearts and corrode the foundation of our souls. Finally, there is *boiling* anger, which tries to find ways to avenge the wrongs done to us. We may try to settle the matters on our own, forgetting that God has promised, "Vengeance is mine; I will re-pay, says the Lord" (Romans 12:19, NRSVUE).

Some people have lived under such tyrannical oppression, have been the victims of such unreasonable tragedy and loss, or have been affected by their own brain chemistry such that living as their truest selves seems unreachable and impossible. These individuals need permission to express their anger—even to explode, perhaps, and let out their deepest, most honest emotions in an effort to liberate their souls. But because anger is a potent emotion, we must learn to redirect and channel it properly. Rather than making people the target of our anger, we must learn to offer up the anger built up inside of us to God. So we pray, "Lord, you see my anger. I am angry with you. I am angry with my friends. I am angry with these lead-ers. I am angry with so-and-so. I do not want to carry this anger any longer, so I consecrate it and give it to you."

Consecration is a fancy word theologians like to use that simply means to dedicate something to God so he may use it for his purposes. We think we have to dedicate to God only what is good and gracious in us, but God also wants us to offer to him the ugly, broken, unpleasant parts of our selves we wish to hide away in closets. God actually wants those parts of our selves more so he can teach us how to redirect our anger to what makes *him* angry: injustices in this world and hidden sin.

Grieving Well

During our earthly existence we will encounter loss. Loss can come in all varieties—relationships, opportunities, spouses, jobs, children, mental capacities, physical health, and more. We live in a broken world that affects us at every level and every turn. Experiencing loss is never fun, especially when it is someone we love or something that is valuable to us. We might encounter guilt along this path. Guilt often visits us with its cousins *regret* and *remorse*. We might carry a sense of remorse for things we did that might have contributed to our loss. We might also carry a sense of regret for the things we failed to do in the past. But there is hope for us. The Word says, "Therefore there is now no condemnation for those who are in Christ Jesus" (Romans 8:1). This is good news for us!

Grieving well is hard work. After my husband passed away from brain cancer in the middle of the pandemic of 2020, I had a choice to make. I could either let my pain take over, or I could try to take over my pain. At first the pain was unbearable, but it subsided little by little and eventually became more manageable. I am grateful for my community of faith, but I am also grateful for my neighbors, some of them who profess no faith but were so kind and caring, mowing my lawn, bringing me meals, and motivating me to join a local cycling club. I had not been physically active for more than three years because I was enrolled in a PhD program, had been taking care of our small children, and had also been caring for my husband during his cancer treatments. So I joined the cycling club and eventually began to train for triathlons. Seven months later, I completed my first Half Ironman.

Engaging in competition again brought back a part of myself I had been forgetting to feed, and it gave me a sense of accomplishment and fulfillment. I literally worked out my grief every day in the pool, on the road, and on the bike. I met new people but also stayed close to my circle of friends who had been so helpful to me during the years of my husband's battle with cancer. I also traveled to many of the places that held great significance to us both, where we had shared beautiful times together. I traveled to Kentucky, where we purchased our first home and pastored our first church. I visited Tennessee with my children and friends, a place where we often went on vacation. I trekked to Colorado to visit family and journeyed to Florida, where we spent our honeymoon and every Christmas during our marriage. In short, I took the first year to remember, relive the good memories, and make new ones.

Making the effort to engage in things that make us come alive is how we learn to grieve well. Sometimes we may not have the monetary resources to travel or the energy to enroll in competitions, but most of the time we can find *something* productive to do that will help us grieve well, and choose where to invest our resources so that later we may reap the benefits.

Grieving well also recognizes that sorrow and joy can dwell together and become lifelong companions. Surely there is something to be gained from every loss. Even when the loss is despairing, disheartening, or devastating and the journey toward recovery and restoration is arduous and long, the time will come when the road ahead becomes clear once again. Even if we walk in "a long obedience in the same direction," to borrow Eugene Peterson's phrase, we will soon realize that walking in "the same direction" does not mean walking a straight line. There will be valleys of sorrow and mountains of difficulty. There will be twisty turns and dry wastelands. Without a doubt, there will be seasons of grief along the way. But, as the hymn "God Will Take Care of You" says:

Be not dismayed whate'er betide; God will take care of you.
Beneath his wings of love abide, God will take care of you.

> Thro' days of toil when heart doth fail,
> God will take care of you.
> When dangers fierce your path assail,
> God will take care of you.

All you may need he will provide; God will take care of you.
Nothing you ask will be denied; God will take care of you.

No matter what will be the test, God will take care of you.
Lean, weary one, upon his breast; God will take care of you.

(Refrain)

God will take care of you, thro' ev'ry day, o'er all the way.

He will take care of you; God will take care of you.[3]

So lean in. Let the tears come, and let laughter bring you back up. Do it all holding on to him who sees your pain, knows your hurt, and understands your heart. For God too has suffered loss, and his Son was also acquainted with sorrow and grief. Grief is not the end. Life does not have to be about the losses we face. Grief can be a gateway into the experience of compassion and empathy, connecting us to the larger reality of the human race.

Keeping Pride Away

The Puritans used to say that pride is the last thing to leave the heart and the first thing to return to it. And pride comes in many varieties and flavors. There is the arrogant type, which always thinks, *I know more* and that everyone ought to listen. There is the superior kind, which thinks, *I am better than anyone else, and I should be recognized for my abilities, skills, and knowledge.* And there is the subtler kind found among many of us, which says, *I will do it my way.* This last type is the most perilous of all, for it keeps God away from directing our lives. But once we relinquish our control, we will find that God was

---

3. Civilla D. Martin (words, 1904) and W. Stillman Martin (music, 1904), "God Will Take Care of You," *Sing to the Lord* (Kansas City, MO: Lillenas Publishing Company, 1993), #107.

looking for a place to dwell so he could bring back to life what was dead and enliven what he has already deposited in us: our passions, talents, gifts, and desires. All these beautiful things have been uniquely shaped and designed by God so we may flourish as individuals. Giving up control does not make us puppets, nor does it make us glorified. It simply brings us to the place of surrender so we may find the purity and power to step into our purpose with the kind of assurance and confidence that we can only obtain by laying down our lives.

Deep Calls unto Deep

Going deeper into the mysteries of God requires that we also go lower. We cannot find and meet the richness and blessings of God if we only go deeper. We must also submerge ourselves in the depths of the waters of his Spirit. Just like the treasures of the ocean can be found the deeper and lower we go, so the treasures of the kingdom of God can be appropriated this way. Theologian W. H. Vanstone once remarked that the church is like a swimming pool in which all the noise comes from the shallow end—but most of the treasures are found in the deep end. If we are to love and live like Jesus, we need the love of Jesus to sustain us, and his love is richer the deeper we submerge ourselves in the waters of his Spirit.

Jesus loved his disciples so deeply that, even though he knew they would variously betray, deny, and desert him, he still chose to serve them. Jesus was able to love these rugged, simple-hearted, unsophisticated disciples despite their shortcomings because he had banked his faith on the Father's love. His security and identity were anchored in the reality of the Father's love for him; as a result, he could extend it freely to others. When Jesus knew the hour had come for him to journey back to his Father, he displayed his deepest sense of love for his disciples in a menial, ordinary way. As Jesus got up from the Passover meal, he took off his outer robe, wrapped a towel around his waist, and bent down to wash the dust-covered, filthy feet of his disciples. Jesus's example shows us three steps we must all take in order to be transformed spiritually.

First, we must nurture a deliberate *disposition* in our hearts to love well, breaking away from the mundane tasks that demand most of our time and distract us from our primary calling as partners in the mission of God. Jesus showed the importance of this first step when he "got up from the meal" to serve his disciples (John 13:4). By making a conscious effort to leave his place of comfort at the table, he prepared his heart to participate in an act of service, pouring water into a basin after he partook of a meal with his disciples. Similarly, we must make time to care for our souls in ways that are life-giving, both individually and communally while fostering an attitude of readiness for service.

Second, we must embrace a radical posture of *dispossession.* When Jesus "took off his outer clothing" (v. 4), he demonstrated the necessity of choosing to become vulnerable, to be real, and to shy away from a performance-oriented, pride-enabling, power-driven type of ministry. This intentional exposure and profound uncovering invites us to develop resilient hearts that can withstand the lures of familiar temptations. In the midst of twists and turns, opportunities for self-advancement, or life's many unexpected hurts, we will be able to step into authenticity by taking the less-traveled road of vulnerability, openness, honesty, and confession. The dispossession of the self is far from simplistic. It requires our coming to God with no pretense and being willing to offer him all we can give, which is really all he wants: our broken selves. This is not always easy when we think we have to have it all together, or when we think somehow we have arrived and no longer need to offer ourselves to him, or when we have been deeply wounded. It takes time to relinquish our need for control, and it takes courage to release our deepest pain. But God's grace makes release possible, and his grace invites us to embark on this process one step at a time. In doing so, the fragmented parts of ourselves may be saturated by his life-giving Spirit.

Finally, we must faithfully engage in a lifestyle of *dispensation.* Just as Jesus "began to wash his disciples' feet, drying them with the towel that was wrapped around him" (v. 5), so must we participate in tangible demonstrations of God's love for those around us. The graces and gifts we have received are to be carefully unwrapped so we may dry the tears of those who mourn and celebrate with those who rejoice. As we put to use the gifts we have received, we do so that others may come "to grasp how wide and long and high and deep is the love of Christ" for us (Ephesians 3:18). Our own journey into the depths of God's love will provide the catalyst we need for spiritual transformation. This experience of deep spiritual healing and transformation lived and demonstrated by Christians is what our world needs the most today.

A spirituality that hides in a cocoon, seeking to protect itself from all possible perils, will likely wither and die in the valley of self-preservation. On the other hand, a spirituality that is marked by caring excessively for those who don't need it, by perfectionism, or by exaggerated activism will sooner or later crumble and collapse on the mountain of self-reliance. Only by cultivating dependence on the Father and embracing an attitude of interdependence will we swim freely in the currents of God's love.

God's saving works are always universal in dimension but particular in function. If God desires to rescue, redeem, purify, and sanctify the world, God must first mold and conform his people to his purposes. God is concerned with rescuing and restoring a fallen creation in order to bring glory to his name. God calls his church to bear witness to the in-breaking of his kingdom in many different ways, starting with surrendering to his will and abandoning to his grace. The question remains, however: how can we, who have witnessed and become the recipients of the new reality of God's transforming grace, partner with him in this adventure? The answer is, by simply uniting our hearts with God's in purpose. The mission of God belongs *to* God, and we are simply invited to share and participate in his plans. As we plead with God through persevering supplication for the removal of obstacles, known or unknown, we are brought to a state of utter dependence, of entire surrender to him and therefore to union with him, so that whatever hinders us may be ultimately overcome by the power of his presence.

I wrote this poem during one of those nights when my soul was in anguish, thirsting for reawakening. I hope its words become a blessing to those who read them.

A Torn Leaf

The trees are naked, the birds away
The wind blows, the branches sway
Shaped in many forms, except round
A torn leaf falls on the ground

A pale soul; a broken vase; a heart in pain
Nothing can wash it away—not even the rain
Without fearing what memories may bring
You close your eyes and start to dream

There is no room for impediments
Will you allow it to become mere sediments?
Your soul emits an unknown sound
But it flew away and is no longer found

Raindrops fall on the ground
Distilling the dormant grass all around
It drenches the body of the torn leaf
Reviving its dullness with relief

The torn leaf is no longer alone
Deeply grounded, it will not be blown
It shall contribute to a fertile ground
Being too vital to remain bound

PART II

INTERCESSORY PRAYER

"Prayer is one of our most deadly and effective weapons for destroying the works of the enemy. Prayer is God's lifeline to the hurting, the wounded, the weak, and the dying."
— James Goll, *The Lost Art of Intercession*

❊ ❊ ❊

"It is in intercession for others that our faith and love and perseverance will be aroused, and that power of the Spirit be found which can fit us for saving men."
— Andrew Murray, *The Ministry of Intercession*

❊ ❊ ❊

"True intercession is actually twofold. One aspect is asking God for divine intervention; the other is destroying the works of Satan."
— Cindy Jacobs, *Possessing the Gates of the Enemy*

❊ ❊ ❊

"Intercessory prayer is the purifying bath into which the individual and the fellowship must enter every day."
— Dietrich Bonhoeffer, *Life Together*

❊ ❊ ❊

"Intercessory prayer is priestly ministry, and one of the most challenging teachings in the New Testament is the universal priesthood of all Christians."
— Richard Foster, *Prayer*

4 ✳ JESUS, OUR MODEL FOR PRAYER

There is no one who modeled a life of continual prayer and intercession like Jesus himself. Jesus prayed in the mornings, spent entire nights talking with his Father, and taught others how to pray. Prayer was his very lifeline. It was the way by which he refueled his tank in order to carry out his ministry obligations day after day. Andrew Murray says, "God took his own Son and made him our example."[1] It seems impossible for us to imitate the Son of God because we feel inadequate at the thought that we could ever be like him. Jesus's life of prayer and times of intercession seem to be both the hallmark of his power and the energizing force that allowed him to be able to stay focused on his mission. In the fellowship of his sufferings, the simplicity and boldness of faith, and the endurance to pre-

---

1. Andrew Murray, *The Ministry of Intercession: A Plea for More Prayer* (Abbotsford, WI: Aneko Press, 2016), 107.

vail and endure all things, Christ offers to help us day by day if we are simply willing to learn from him how to pray.

The Praying God-Man

Jesus left his glorious abode in heaven to become incarnate in human flesh. This immersion into the earthly realm became the setting where he acquired the sensitivity to understand humanity, the opportunity to encounter people, and the desire to engage in the culture around him with joy and zest. Jesus attended funerals and weddings. He attended religious festivals and observances and participated in rituals. He did not escape the world. He engaged others in their daily activities, routines, tasks, and work. He enjoyed being with people so much that he specifically invited twelve ordinary men to follow him and learn from him and minister with him. Many others followed him of their own accord, like Nicodemus and Joseph of Arimathea, who were both secret disciples (John 3:1–2; 19:38); and Mary Magdalene, Joanna, and Susanna, who were so invested in Jesus's mission and ministry that they supported him "out of their own means" (Luke 8:3). Jesus laughed and wept with people. He recognized that humanity was both beautiful and frail—therefore, he knew humans needed a savior to bring them into the full-fledged maturity of their beauty.

But Jesus knew he could do nothing apart from the Father. And, although Jesus was without sin, he became subject to every temptation known to humankind, overcoming each one by the Word and the Spirit (see Matthew 4:1–11; Mark 1:9–13; Luke 4:1–13). He showed us that the way to overcome temptation, trial, and tribulation is through dependence on the Father, fellowship with the Spirit, and community with others. Because Jesus was God made flesh, it would be easy for us to think he had an advantage when it came to prayer. But let's think about it. He was a busy man. His schedule was always full. Large crowds gathered to hear his teachings. Many went out of their way to beg for his healing. Yet, in the midst of his strenuous itinerary, he found time to be alone and retreat to solitary places in order to get recharged and connect with his Father. He needed time away from others in order to be able to pour himself into others. Even when people looked for him and tried to keep him from leaving, he was adamant about going to solitary places or spending entire nights away praying (see Luke 4:42–43; 6:12; 11:1). Jesus prayed before making decisions (Luke 6:12–13). He prayed before performing miracles (John 11:41–44). And he prayed before being arrested (Luke 22:39–46; John 17).

Of course, many of us love to hear, study, and memorize the words of Jesus, but few of us dare to live the kind of audacious life, fueled by intimacy with the Father, that Jesus lived. Jesus lived a life of daily surrender for the sake of the world. He lived a life of costly love, daring faith, and dauntless hope against all hope. This kind of life was possible because Jesus recognized the transience of earthly life. He was just passing by. This transient ground between the reality of our present difficulties and our coming victory should propel us, motivate us, and prompt us to a deeper life of prayer, as it did for Jesus. Similarly, the recognition that this life is temporary should beckon us not to set our hearts on the accumulation of wealth. Setting our hearts on what is unseen, while living amidst the harsh reality of what is seen, reminds us that, like Jesus, we are simply passing through this earthly life.

The transient ground on which we live is often accompanied by concomitant feelings of insecurity and confidence, misfortune and serendipity, conflict and contentment, gales of sorrow and trees of joy. For what perishes blossoms, and what blossoms perishes, but that which has purpose cannot be feared or ignored; it must be believed, and it must be lived on. The secret is to learn to live in this transient space with hopeful expectation of what is yet to come. Jesus demonstrated this knowledge in his darkest hour. He carried in tension the dismaying weight of doubt as he prayed, "My God, my God, why have you forsaken me?" (Matthew 27:46) along with the relentless delight of trust when he cried out, "Father, into your hands I commit my spirit" (Luke 23:46). The same hour of darkness invited doubt and trust to intermingle, but trust won as he drew his last breath and declared, "It is finished" (John 19:30).

The praying God-man knew humanity would be buffeted by external circumstances that would encumber the bliss of life. He himself was buffeted by external circumstances, but it did not deter him from fulfilling the purpose and mission for which he was sent. He also knew that battles would give us the opportunity to overcome, that conflict would offer us the chance to seek resolution, and that we could learn to survive in the struggle. He himself said, "Blessed are you who are poor, for yours is the kingdom of God. Blessed are you who hunger now, for you will be satisfied. Blessed are you who weep now, for you will laugh" (Luke 6:20–21). The transience of our momentary experience on earth ebbs back and forth between what once was and what is not fully yet. And that's the reason Jesus *still* prays—so that we may come closer to the reality that is found in him. Because he is our faithful intercessor who lives to pray for us, we can rest assured that, even in moments when we are frail, even when we are unable to pray, and even in seasons when we might not *want* to pray, he is praying for us (Hebrews 7:25).

The Prayers of Jesus

A quick look at the Gospel narratives will give us insight into the heart of Jesus and the breadth and depth of the prayers he prayed. Without a particular order of priority, I here classify his prayers in a way that might help us put them into practice.

The Prayer of Gratitude

The prayer of gratitude tends to be neglected in Christian practice, whether because we forget about it altogether or we might consider it inferior to the other kinds of prayer. But when prayer is both the duty *and* the delight of the human community, it becomes a response to God's grace, and we show that response best through gratitude and praise. An example of this type of prayer from Jesus is found in John 11, when Jesus became deeply moved at the place of the tomb where Lazarus had been for four days. Whether he was moved because Lazarus was a good friend or because the event foreshadowed Jesus's own finality as a human being, it is hard to say. What we do know from the text is that Jesus said his prayer of gratitude out loud as he prepared to raise Lazarus: "Father, I thank you that you have heard me. I knew that you always hear me, but I said this for the benefit of the people standing here, that they may believe that you sent me" (vv. 41–42). In this simple prayer, Jesus demonstrated how gratitude is deeply connected to what we need and therefore should always guide our evocations in preparation for what we ought to receive.

When Jesus thanks the Father for hearing his request, he is affirming that his Father is not aloof, sitting in his heavenly abode and watching the world operate like a machine. Jesus's prayer reinforces the idea that God the Father is intricately involved in the affairs of the world and cares deeply about our needs, whether little or big. In this way, the prayer of gratitude takes a position of *confidence* in the greatness and goodness of God.

Jesus's prayer at the tomb of Lazarus also affirms that our prayers of gratitude do not have to wait until after we receive an answer to what we have asked. Instead, our prayers of gratitude can be *anticipatory*. Jesus thanks the Father for hearing him and *then* commands Lazarus to come out—and he does. When we pray, we should thank God ahead of time for what God is going to do, even though we might not know what God will do. We might pattern our prayer in a similar fashion to what Jesus prayed, saying, "Father I thank you that you have heard me and that you will grant this request in your time and in your way." Praying this way allows our minds to be filled with peace rather than worry. Instead of asking God to do this or that and doubting whether God will, we pray with gratitude and confidence for what is to come.

Finally, the prayer of gratitude is *purposeful*. Right after Jesus thanks the Father, he mentions that he does it for the benefit of the people. So, when we pray, we can be thankful for the way God will channel the answer to our prayers as a sign and mark of blessing so that the world may come to know him through what he has given us. Through this faithful response of thanksgiving, we find the joy to carry on even when the answers to our prayers feel delayed or come in a different way than expected.

The Prayer of Lament

Even if prayers have undertones of thanksgiving, that does not preclude them from being laments. This juxtaposition is clearly seen in the worship of the Israelites. In Psalms, for instance, we find a collection of prayers and hymns that reveal the necessity of wailing and moaning as a result of fallen earthly circumstances while also embracing God's sovereignty and future providence as a sign of promise. These prayers of lament serve as a cathartic release and opportunity to encounter God in solidarity with those who suffer or those who remain far from the presence of God. The process of wailing does not make painful realities cease, nor do past grievances magically disappear from memory. Wailing allows the people of God to express their suffering as a part of their ongoing relationship between God and their fellow humans.

We also find Jesus expressing the faith of his hurting soul through lament, expressed as sorrow for the city and people of Jerusalem. Although this prayer is not formally directed to God, it is a prayer nonetheless, since it mourns the areas in the world that remain absent of any recognition of God's presence: "Jerusalem, Jerusalem, you who kill the prophets and stone those sent to you, how often I have longed to gather your children together, as a hen gathers her chicks under her wings, and you were not willing. Look, your house is left to you desolate. I tell you, you will not see me again until you say, 'Blessed is he who comes in the name of the Lord'" (Luke 13:34–35). Jesus was clearly troubled over the way the people of Jerusalem allowed injustice and cruelty to dictate their steps, choosing destructive ways instead of the ways of God. Jesus recognized that such actions would lead to the desolation of their people. Jesus lamented their choosing of their own evil ways instead of his.

Hebrews 5:7 says, "During the days of Jesus' life on earth, he offered up prayers and petitions with fervent cries and tears to the one who could save him from death, and he was heard because of his reverent submission." Shedding tears in our prayers reflects the condition of a heart that is soft, gentle, caring, and forbearing. The language of lament seems to have been removed from much of contemporary worship today, yet throughout the Psalter as well as in Jesus's own prayers, we find that lament serves as a sign of confessional maturity and solidarity with those who have been victims of trauma, oppression, or injustice. The prayer of lament is both personal and communal. It is an outlet of worship that invites us to groan, weep, and release our pain in recognition that the Spirit of God is also interceding for us with groans that words cannot express (Romans 8:26). Thus, we may approach God with confidence and find comfort when we join our tears with those who weep and unite our sighs with those who mourn.

The Prayer of Surrender

The prayer of surrender is best described as a silent consecration of our ambitions and a relinquishment of our own capricious will. The best example is Jesus's prayer in Gethsemane before he was arrested: "Father, if you are willing, take this cup from me; yet not my will, but yours be done" (Luke 22:42). The prayer of surrender is not an easy prayer. Jesus's own experience of anguish shows us that surrendering our will to God's is costly. It might cost us time. It might require tears. But once we join Jesus in surrendering our will to the Father's, we may find that choosing his will brings our self-sufficiency to an end, empowering us with greater energy to be able to choose what is right, virtuous, noble, and good with freedom and confidence.

The prayer of surrender may be a one-time deal, or it may have to be repeated over and over until we find the object of our surrender completely released from our grip. Surrendering is unnatural. We like to win. We like to succeed. We like to compete for more and bigger and better. But the way up is the way down. The more we release and surrender, the more room we make for God to to enact his will and mission through us. Sometimes we may not know what exactly to surrender. So we invite God to guide us and show us the obstacles that seem to be hindering his indwelling presence. It could be something as small as a habit or as big as a life-altering decision. The moment we surrender, we arrive at the station of acceptance, which slowly liberates us from the prison of comparison, the chains of discontentment, and the dungeon of despair.

The Prayer for Protection

Praying for protection is not a magic formula or supernatural force we can harness that will keep us from experiencing pain, harm, or difficulty. Sometimes the answers to our prayers for protection come in the form of peace, strength, courage, and determination to keep going in the middle of despair. When Jesus prayed for his disciples, he said,

I will remain in the world no longer, but they are still in the world, and I am coming to you. Holy Father, protect them by the power of your name, the name you gave me, so that they may be one as we are one. While I was with them, I protected them and kept them safe by that name you gave me. None has been lost except the one doomed to destruction so that Scripture would be fulfilled. . . . My prayer is not that you take them out of the world but that you protect them from the evil one.
(John 17:11–12, 15)

The protection that Jesus offers us comes in the form of love and provision in the face of adversity, calamity, and temptation. When we pray for protection, we are not praying for God to keep all adversity away. Rather, we are asking God to be with us through the inevitable troubles we know we will experience. As Psalm 34:19 says, "The righteous person may have many troubles, but the LORD delivers him from them all." It would be impossible to live a completely safe, unharmed, and unhindered life on this side of eternity. Jesus himself experienced trouble, adversity, persecution. But his faith, trust, and steadfastness remained constant until the end.

Praying for protection implies our confidence in God's provision. Rather than praying, "God, protect me from harm," we should say, "Thank you, Lord, for protecting and keeping me regardless of what may come." That way, instead of growing frustrated when something bad happens because God did not answer our prayer, we prepare ourselves for the situations we may have to face with a mentality that defies obstacles, overcomes hurdles, and defeats the arrows of the enemy that are sent to deflate our faith and discourage us along the way. It is with this type of confidence and assurance that Paul, Silas, and Timothy affirmed, "But the Lord is faithful, and he will strengthen and protect you from the evil one" (2 Thessalonians 3:3).

The Prayer for Unity

Prayer reveals our deepest longings. It is a conversation that God started, and we get to continue it as we express our innermost desires to him. We see a glimpse of Jesus's desires and longing for his children when he prays for all the believers to be one and to be brought to complete unity, with the objective that the world may know the Father's love (John 17:21, 23).

The unity that Jesus prays his children would attain does not mean *uniformity of thought*. Uniformity would be impossible because all of God's children come from different traditions, cultural backgrounds, and lifestyles and have formed unique preferences and spiritual habits that have been shaped by their time, generation, and cultural upbringing. Jesus does not expect us to lose our personalities or our cultural distinctions. Diversity must be celebrated with purity of heart, recognizing that the other has something to share and contribute that can be helpful to enlarge our understanding. Neither does the unity Christ desires imply *uniformity of action*. Christians are called to different tasks and ministries because each person is wired uniquely and has been given particular gifts and talents to exercise particular assignments and callings.

The unity that Christ desires is one of heart and purpose—so that the world may know that he is the Christ and that the Father loves each and every one of us. The unity Jesus prays for is attainable only when we lay down our lives and our preferences to take up his cross for his redemptive purposes.

The Focus of the Lord's Prayer

The world craves true spiritual connection, and Jesus provides us a pattern by which we can experience it through the Lord's Prayer. This prayer may be singlehandedly the most spoken, memorized, and recited prayer of all the prayers found in the Bible. But, as American theologian and pastor Timothy Keller points out, this prayer "is an untapped resource, partially because it is so very familiar."[2] When we pray this prayer with our heads—that is, without aligning our hearts with its petitions—the words may be devoid of true reflection and meaning. But when we invite our hearts to participate in this prayer, a well of treasure may be uncovered. Recognizing the many aspects of this prayer will help us formulate a better understanding of Jesus's instruction and invitation to journey through a richer engagement with our Lord himself.

Invocation: *Our Father in Heaven*

The opening line of the Lord's Prayer shows us two important theological understandings about prayer. First, the opening words of this prayer are communal and not individual. Although it is of utmost importance to practice times of personal-individual prayer, its communal aspect must not be ignored. The Lord himself emphasizes how we are to direct *our* prayer to *our* God.

Second, we are addressing the Father in heaven, who is not bound by gender, location, space, or time. We are told to pray to the Father as a way to understand our own relationship to the triune God. We are the children, and God is the One

---

2. Timothy Keller, *Prayer: Experiencing Awe and Intimacy with God* (New York: Penguin Books, 2014), 109.

who provides, nurtures, and cares for us. Heaven is his abiding place, just like our hearts may become his abiding place. He lives in eternal glory, surrounded by unapproachable light, in radiant splendor, and he invites us to experience glimpses of his glory here on earth.

Adoration: *Hallowed Be Your Name*

Why would it be important to affirm that God's name is "hallowed?" What does it mean to *hallow* God? It simply means we honor him for who he is: holy in his perfect Trinity. Adoration is the gateway into God's presence, and we can only enter by ducking our heads as we walk through the low doors of humility. We recognize that we are not able to approach him in his glory, but through Jesus Christ we can approach with confidence and assurance. So we worship and praise and thank him. This attitude allows our hearts to prepare for what is to come—recognizing his faithfulness for what he has already done. We recognize that his name is above every other name and is indeed worthy to receive all praise. Adoration comes first because it heals the heart of its self-centeredness.

Restoration: *Your Kingdom Come*

When we pray for God's kingdom to come, we are actually praying for God's rule over all aspects of life. But when we serve our own goals, ambitions, and agendas, God cannot rule over the spiritual, psychological, cultural, and material problems we face.

God's kingdom comes in three ways. First, it comes through his *Spirit*, who redirects our desires. Second, it comes through his *Word*, which restructures our thoughts. Third, it comes through his *people*, who reshape our individual priorities in life.

When we pray for God's kingdom to come, we pray for his lordship over our lives and affairs. We are asking God to extend his dominion over every part of our lives, which requires us to transfer our allegiance from the earthly economy to God's economy of redemption. Although the reign of God is only partial right now on this earth, we can have a simple taste through his church and his Spirit. The fullness of his kingdom shall be revealed one day when all suffering, pain, poverty, illness, and death shall end. Yearning for God's kingdom invites us to reimagine a world where peace, justice, and love govern over the ailments and disorders of our present world.

Forbearance: *Your Will Be Done*

This petition is founded on two fronts—first, the present necessity for grace to sustain us in times of difficulty and uncertainty; second, the future desire for grace to restore and heal what is broken. It is surely easy to pray, "your will be done" when God's will and our will are aligned. But as we encounter forks along the road that force us to make difficult decisions, praying for God's will to be done may not prove appealing. Following God always leads to the best results, even if the process seems painful. One would think that keeping this truth in mind would make it as easy to implement as it is to entertain, but every time my will collides with God's will, I am faced with the same dilemma: whether to follow God or to pursue my own desires.

What if there were a middle way? What if, rather than wishing God would side with my will or reluctantly deciding to follow God's will, I learned to accept what God allows in his permissive will to bring about his perfect will for me? Could it be that praying for God's will to be done—whether I am well fed or hungry, whether I am living in poverty or bounty, whether I am in chains or in a free land—is truly asking for God's liberation, restoration, healing, and salvation? Could it be that it requires a faithful stewardship of the resources he has given us, regardless of the cost? Praying for his will to be done is risky, but ultimately it is the best prayer, for we trust that he is turning things around and making all things new.

Provision: *Our Daily Bread*

After we recognize God as the source of life and nourishment, we petition for our needs to be met according to God's riches. Praying for daily bread entails asking God for our necessities rather than extravagances, and for sustenance and justice for all. How can we get our daily bread if we refuse to share what we already have? To pray this prayer is to pray against exploitation in the economic sector, which often deprives others from their own daily bread. To pray for our daily bread is not for the bread to remain in the confinements of our own personal enjoyment but to receive what we need on a daily basis in order to become channels of blessing to others.

Release: *Forgive Us as We forgive Others*

This petition is perhaps the most difficult of all of the petitions in the Lord's Prayer. The river of grace can only run unhindered through the gift of forgiveness. Regular confession liberates the heart of its deadly poison. Forgiving those who have judged us, hurt us, misunderstood us, and cursed us makes us great candidates for God's continual forgiveness to come to us when we are the ones who judge, misunderstand, or hurt others.

It has been said that bitterness is like drinking poison and expecting the other person to die from it. Forgiving someone who has caused a deep wound or been the perpetrator of injustice is not easy, but it is the only way to liberate the soul from potential blockages and free the heart from the shackles of vengeance. Forgiveness is not forgetting, but it is letting go of our resentment. Forgiveness is a complex process that takes time. Forgiveness does not mean we received an apology. It simply means the grievance no longer remains a barrier to the relationship. We may still feel some pain related to the past, but when we release forgiveness, the anger inside of us toward that person or situation subsides.

A story I heard once may help to illuminate the importance of releasing old hurts so that we may move with freedom and purpose, asking God to do for us what we have been willing to do for others.

Long ago, two monks were traveling on foot and came to a swiftly moving river. A woman who was standing alone on the bank approached the monks and asked if they could help her cross so she could return home to her family. Knowing it was forbidden to touch a woman, one monk looked the other way, ignoring her request for help. The other monk, feeling compassion for the desperate lady, decided to bend the rules. Breaking tradition, he lifted her into his arms and carried her safely across the rushing water.

Exceedingly grateful, the lady thanked the helpful monk and went home. The two monks continued on their journey.

After walking some miles in silence, the first monk finally looked at the other and said, "I can't believe you carried that woman! You know we're never supposed to touch the opposite sex."

The other monk replied, "Well, that is interesting. I set that woman down many miles ago, but you continue to carry her in your heart."

Guidance: *Lead Us Not into Temptation*

It is strange that Jesus would invite us to pray this type of prayer. It almost seems confounding and strange to ask God not to lead us toward something into which he clearly does not want us to fall. However, this statement reveals the depth of trust inherent in the petition. If we pray not to be led to a place where God already does not want us to go, we then walk through life with the assurance that we are being guided by God's hand and held by his grace—regardless of where life takes us. This prayer involves the recognition that we will experience times of trials and testing, which are inevitable in life and also serve the purpose of making us more humble, durable, faithful, and loving.

There are three categories of temptations that we should guard against and ask God to help us avoid. First is the temptation of *incredulity*. Incredulity occurs when we hear the word of God but confusion, doubt, and ignorance begin to corrode the basis of our faith, causing us to be led away from the source of true life because we no longer believe. The second type of temptation is *success*—for example, when riches, power, and honor tempt us to think we are self-reliant and no longer need God for our daily sustenance. The third type of temptation can be labeled *misfortune*. It occurs when poverty, suffering, adversity, and afflictions tempt us to despair, to lose hope, and to become alienated from God.

Asking God to lead us not into temptation, then, is a petition that is bathed in the waters of purification that cleanse us from the evils inside of us that might lead us astray.

Deliverance: *Deliver Us from the Evil One*

This petition is a cry for liberation from the evils that emanate from the kingdom of the ruler of the air: Satan. This cry is an appeal for God's rescuing power to free us from the deadly threats of sickness, dishonor, poverty, disorder, and brokenness. Although we cannot be fully free in this life from the malignant forces operating in the world, our prayer for deliverance and protection against the enemy's schemes finds an appropriate place in the Lord's Prayer. Therefore, we would be wise to emphasize the petition and extend it to all areas of life, from our family members to our job opportunities to our bodily welfare.

Jesus's pattern and focus of prayer show us the essence of the faith. First, we ought to glorify God and enjoy his presence. Second, we ought to trust him as we petition for our provision and protection. Jesus's revolutionary prayer truly serves as a skeleton we can use as a basis to formulate our own daily prayers.

5 ✳ THE MINISTRY OF INTERCESSION

Prayer is like fuel, providing us with the necessary energy to keep going. Without filling the gas tank, the car might start, but it will not go very far. For the church to be effective in evangelism and disciple-making, intercession must be its main lifeline. From the shared experiences of numerous missionaries and revivalists around the world, we would do well to remember that formulas, methods, and strategies will prove insufficient unless we understand the urgency of intercession for lost souls and for the full redemption and restoration of our brokenness. Intercession clearly shows us that God's chosen people do not live for ourselves. By humbling ourselves in dependence upon the Father and carrying one another's burdens, we realize that we "exist for the sake of God's glory and his mission, and for the sake of others toward whom God's mission is directed."[1]

---

1. Michael W. Goheen, *A Light to the Nations: The Missional Church and the Biblical Story* (Grand Rapids: Baker Academic, 2011), 26.

Intercession is one of the most vital tasks of our lives, yet it is rarely the *only* task. Proclaiming the liberating news of the gospel, reaching out to the destitute through acts of kindness, loving mercy, seeking justice, and striving for unity in the body of Christ are all examples that illustrate how Christians ought to be oriented toward God, toward others, and toward the environment that sustains human life. Nevertheless, intercession is perhaps one of the most neglected, least emphasized, and quickly aborted ministries. This chapter will present the ways that the ministry of intercession can make an impact in the world by surveying the contributions of key individuals throughout history who were called to this venture.

Prevailing Prayer

We find men and women in the Bible who walked with God and had an intimate relationship with him. The Bible records many great accomplishments for the kingdom of God that came as a result of fervent, incessant, intercessory prayer. Prayer is not only a weapon, a force, and a sign; it is also the language of our soul. Without prayer, our spirit becomes frail, weak, powerless, and cold. God has given us the keys to the kingdom, and his kingdom blessings can only be unlocked by intercessory prayer. Throughout biblical history, men and women who turned their worlds upside down for Christ were gripped by the vision of prevailing prayer. The promises they obtained, the powers of darkness they subdued, and the transformation of lives they facilitated did not come by strategies or programs but as a result of sacrificial, intercessory, costly prayer that then moved them to be the holy representatives of God in a broken world.

Let's consider Abraham, who moved on God when God was about to destroy Sodom for their great sin. Abraham said to God, "Far be it from you to do such a thing—to kill the righteous with the wicked, treating the righteous and the wicked alike. Far be it from you! Will not the Judge of all the earth do right?" (Genesis 18:25). And every time Abraham gave God a new number, Abraham received what he pleaded for. Perhaps the whole land could have been spared if he had kept asking all the way down to one.

Let's also remember Jacob, who wrestled with an angel all night long and finally declared, "I will not let you go unless you bless me" (Genesis 32:26). Jacob had to have God's blessing! He wouldn't let go until he got it. And he did get it! Jacob was desperate for God's blessings in his life. When we get that desperate in our wrestling in prayer with God, something is likely to happen.

Of course, there is also Moses, who came to God in great consternation after hearing that the Israelites made idols of gold. He exerted his priestly role by interceding on their behalf as he said to God, "Oh, what a great sin these people have committed! They have made themselves gods of gold. But now, please forgive their sin—but if not, then blot me out of the book you have written" (Exodus 32:31–32). Moses was willing to sacrifice his own destiny and eternal security for God to intervene in this situation. And God relented, as confirmed in Psalm 106: "So [God] said he would destroy them—had not Moses, his chosen one, stood in the breach before him to keep his wrath from destroying them" (v. 23).

There are the prophets, whose unique calling involved a life of prayer—Elisha, Jeremiah, Elijah, Ezekiel, and more. The miracles they did, the feats they accomplished, and the legacies they left behind could have never been possible had they not walked closely with their God until the end.

And there were the women, like Esther, who cried out, "If I perish, I perish" (Esther 4:16), but who was willing to go, to fast for her people, to risk her life, whatever the cost. Or Hannah, who year after year wept bitterly and one day in her anguish "made a vow, saying, 'LORD Almighty, if you will only look on your servant's misery and remember me, and not forget your servant but give her a son, then I will give him to the LORD for all the days of his life. . .'" (1 Samuel 1:11). Her request was granted, and her son became one of the greatest figures in the Old Testament, occupying multiple roles as a prophet, high priest, and judge.

Biblical history shows and confirms that nothing of eternal significance is accomplished without prevailing prayer. If there is a lesson to be learned from all these Bible characters, it is the *principle of gravity*: what goes up must come down. As our prayers rise, God's blessings will descend. Thus, intercession is not a gift given only to a select few. Intercession is a privilege and a duty to which all Christians are called. It is one of the most compassionate ministries in which we can participate as we plead with God for intervention and direction on earth.

A Hidden Ministry

There is a legend about a man who was the most powerful king in the world. The legend goes that this king boasted a great army of horses. His trainers learned impressive ways to train the horses, and they became some of the best. In the middle of battle, amid the sounds of clashing swords and the gut-wrenching screams of fallen warriors, the horses were trained to remain sensitive to their riders' commands. The horses learned to respond to many signals, one of which was a whistle. Whenever the whistle was blown, the horses were to instantly come to the king no matter the cost.

After preliminary training, a final test was administered to determine which horse would be the one the king himself rode. All the horses were led into a big corral, and the gate was shut. The horses would be given no food or water for three days. The first day came and went. The horses were certainly hungry, but far worse was their thirst, and many began to run around, trying to find a way to escape. On the second day the horses were famished, but their hunger was nothing compared to their thirst in the middle of such a hot day. Desperately needing water, they attempted to beat down the sides of the fence, fearing they might have been forgotten and left to die. The third day was the same. No food. No water. Now these horses were losing their fight.

Toward the end of the third day, the trainers opened the gate. The horses began to recover a little energy and headed toward the river to quench their thirst. While the horses were running full speed, a trainer blew the king's whistle. Instinctively, the horses stopped, but only for a moment. Almost all of the horses succumbed to their need for water, ignoring the whistle and choosing to satisfy their own needs instead. But a horse of more noble character mustered every ounce of energy available and painfully turned to respond to the whistle. This horse would be the the one the king selected for himself.

Our heavenly King is blowing the whistle. Anyone who hears it and turns to him will be apprehended by the King to do mighty works for him. The King will reveal himself in a unique way and will prepare each of us who responds to the call, until we are made ready to be used for whatever assignment the King has for us in his kingdom.

Principles of Intercession

Initially, prayer requires discipline because it does not come naturally to many, so we must make a conscious effort to practice it. The more we practice, the easier it becomes because we begin to peel off the layers of the self until prayer becomes the language of our souls and, without it, our hearts grow frail and cold. In that way, we will learn to make prayer a rhythmic dance.

Intercession is a specific type of prayer that, at its core, involves carrying other people's burdens and laying them at the foot of the cross. Intercession most clearly reveals to us the depth of God's own compassion for us because he is the One who summons us and deposits specific burdens in our spirits that must be continually released back to him through prayer. Lack of justice and lack of intercession are two things that displease God. As Isaiah the prophet describes: "The LORD looked and was displeased that there was no justice. He saw that there was no one, he was appalled that there was no one to intervene" (59:15b–16a). The word translated "intervene" is the word *paga* in Hebrew, which literally means to "strike the mark" (see Job 36:32). One of the primary meanings for the word *paga* is "to entreat" or "to make intercession." An intercessor is one who makes contact with God, intervening on behalf of the needs of others, carrying their burdens as if they were their own. Interestingly, the word for "sin" in Hebrew is *hata*, which means to "miss the mark." So when we pray for others we hit the mark, but when we become self-focused we miss it. In this process of learning how to hit the mark, we will develop strong spiritual muscles if we do not give up.

The burdens we receive for others must be continually released through prayer, lest they become so heavy that they end up unintentionally crushing us. The closer we are to God, the more we feel his heartbeat for the world. Thus, intercession implies listening to the heart of God for the world—a world often marred by its own deceit and darkness. Rees Howells, one of the greatest intercessors known to history, suggests three levels of intercession.

The first level is *identification*. We might identify with the needs or pain of someone else because we know what it feels like. Perhaps we have been there or shared a similar experience and can relate. At other times, it may be that we identify with the sufferings of Christ so deeply that we are connected to the larger experience of humanity through many shared contexts. Regardless of the reason we sympathize with a specific burden or need, this first level allows us to be truly connected to the other and therefore able to stand in the gap for the person or situation.

The second level is *agony*. When we begin to intercede for others at a deep level, we might feel the heaviness of the situation so deeply that it is as if we were carrying a weighty bag of cement on our shoulders. The agonizing stage might be expressed through groans, tears, sighs, or silence. It is truly feeling the full weight as if it were contained deep inside and expressing it through cries, words, or wordless sounds.

The third level of intercession is *authority*. It is not only connecting and feeling the weight of the situation, but it is also releasing it and taking a position of victory over the burden being carried through prayer. We come to that place of authority once we rest in the assurance that we will see the result of our prayer, even though it might take years before we receive confirmation that the prayer has been answered or see its full evidence in the physical realm.[2]

Potential Dangers of Intercessory Prayer

As a result of an increased awareness of spiritual dynamics, certain trends and strategies have begun to emerge in prayer circles around the world, some controversial and others less so. In the context of Christian mission, awareness of God's role in prayer-centered strategies becomes of paramount importance. Theologies that develop out of zeal cannot be crowned as the ultimate method that births kingdom fruitfulness. It is not prayer itself that does the work but God, who advances his purposes on earth as he finds faithful people who pray.

---

2. All of these levels of intercession are found in Norman Grubb, *Rees Howells, Intercessor: The Story of a Life Lived for God* (Fort Washington, PA: CLC International, 2016), 81.

Despite the tendency toward controversy that some prayer-focused movements seem to have, the increased emphasis on prayer has certainly encouraged the global community of faith to take strides in the right direction. Not only has it made the evangelical church more aware of the urgency of intercession, the importance of corporate prayer, and the reality of the spiritual world, but it has also stimulated the birth of new Spirit-led movements. The panacea, however, does not lie in seeking to develop new methods, strategies, or techniques in order to advance the kingdom of God. Rather, the solution must be found in recovering a heart that seeks to honor God for the sake of his kingdom. A passion for the lost, a longing for God's presence, and the importance of unity in the body of Christ are among the positive elements of prayer-centric movements that should motivate the church to rescue the timeless practice of intercession without falling prey to strategies that prove inadequate.

The development of a balanced and biblical perspective on intercession is essential. Because the intercessor is, in a sense, a mediator between God and a particular situation, the reality of possible spiritual conflict that might ensue cannot be ignored. On the other hand, placing too much emphasis on the power of evil is to lose sight of the reign of Christ. In so doing, we may give the devil too much credit instead of being fully prepared to "resist the devil" (James 4:7) "when the day of evil comes" (Ephesians 6:13). The focus of intercessory prayer must be on the authority that God has given Christians to combat the forces of evil, as well as the power to live a holy life.

A key passage highlighting the intertwinement of these elements is found in Daniel 10. In this passage, Daniel has a vision and mourns what it means for three weeks (vv. 1–2). Then an angel appears to Daniel, apparently in response to three important factors: Daniel's attempt to gain understanding, his humility before God, and his consistency in his prayer life (v. 12). As a result of Daniel's faithfulness, the angel says to him: "Do not be afraid, Daniel. Since the first day that you set your mind to gain understanding and to humble yourself before your God, your words were heard, and I have come in response to them. But the prince of the Persian kingdom resisted me twenty-one days. Then Michael, one of the chief princes, came to help me, because I was detained there with the king of Persia" (vv. 12–13). It is interesting to note that the Hebrew word *melakim* that is translated "king" is actually plural, raising significant questions as to the identity of the "kings" of Persia. While some Bible commentators hold that the author is referring to a group of human kings, others are persuaded that their identity is rooted in the spiritual realm. Stephen R. Miller, for instance, observes, "These 'kings' likely were spiritual rulers who attempted to control Persia," for "the concept of the angel's being 'detained with' the earthly kings of Persia seems untenable."[3]

It is widely held by biblical scholars that each nation was thought to have an angel who served as its protector, acting on behalf of the saints. This perspective is reinforced by the fact that Michael is called a "chief prince" (v. 13), "your prince" (v. 21), the "great prince who protects your people [the Israelites]" (12:1), and is also referred to as the "archangel" in Jude 1:9. Thus, it is possible that the words "prince" and "king" are used interchangeably in this context, leading to the conclusion that the kings and princes who detained Daniel's messenger were dark angels.[4]

This passage would seem to indicate that a cosmic battle between forces of good and evil keeps raging on, involving dark angels wrestling against good angels. These dark forces may exert a certain degree of control over nations, governmental affairs, and people groups (See Deuteronomy 32:8; Psalm 82; Isaiah 24:21). Not all scholars are convinced; some take a less supernatural approach, believing it erroneous to assume that dark spirits ruled over the regions of Persia and Greece. It would be inaccurate, however, to discredit the possibility of

---

3. Stephen R. Miller, *Daniel*, New American Commentary Vol. 18 (Nashville: B&H Publishing Group, 1994), 284.

4. Clinton E. Arnold, *3 Crucial Questions about Spiritual Warfare* (Grand Rapids: Baker Academic, 1997), 154.

a cosmic war raging in the unseen, especially in light of other passages in Scripture that confirm the existence of these beings (see Deuteronomy 32:17; Psalm 96:5; 106:37; Ephesians 1:21; 6:12; 2 Peter 2:10–12; Jude 1:8–10; Revelation 18:2).

Daniel 10 makes no mention of Daniel's desire to seek information regarding the identities, assignments, or locations of these dark forces. Neither does Daniel engage them through prayer with a militant intent to defeat them. Rather, these verses appear to teach us two specific truths that assist us in developing a holistic theology regarding God's role and our role when it comes to intercessory prayer.

First, the aforementioned actions that Daniel models elicit God's response. Daniel set his mind to gain understanding, humbled himself before God, and made earnest intercession for the people of Israel. He was not even aware of the cosmic battle being raged in the heavenly realm, but his petitions were heard as soon as he began to pray (9:23).

Second, the sovereignty, control, and superiority of God are clearly on display, both in this passage and throughout the entire book of Daniel: "He does as he pleases with the powers of heaven" (4:35). God is infinitely higher than anything or any power, and his kingdom will be firmly established throughout the ages: "The God of heaven will set up a kingdom that will never be destroyed" (2:44).

Rather than devoting ourselves to myths that "promote controversial speculations rather than advancing God's work" (1 Timothy 1:4), we must give emphasis to the overarching triumph of God over the created order. We must remember that, although there is a cosmic battle raging in the heavenly realm, there is also certainty about its outcome. While the church expectantly awaits the day when the full restoration of God's creation will finally be realized, we currently live in the tension of the *already* and the *not-yet* of our times. Because the powers of the old age are still present, the old and the new ages will continue to coexist until the day of Christ is fully realized. The church finds itself actively participating in this cosmic battle. Thus, we must be spiritually prepared to resist the oppressive forces of darkness and equipped to stand firm against all forms of evil in both our personal lives and the structural patterns that perpetuate oppressive influences in our societies and ideologies.

6 ❋ THE NEED FOR CORPORATE PRAYER

When Moses' hands grew tired, they took a stone and put it under him and he sat on it. Aaron and Hur held his hands up—one on one side, one on the other—so that his hands remained steady till sunset. So Joshua overcame the Amalekite army with the sword.

—Exodus 17:12-13

I love the story of Moses and Joshua when they headed into battle against the Amalekites. Moses went to the top of a mountain with "the staff of God" (Exodus 17:9) while Joshua went to battle. Moses lifted the staff in supplication to God for the deliverance of Israel, and when his hands were raised, Joshua was able to overcome the Amalekites, but as soon as Moses let his hands down, the Amalekites would begin to prevail. As the day wore on, Moses's energy began to fail, giving the Amalekites the advantage. Aaron and Hur rushed to support Moses, giving him a place to seat and each taking one side to help Moses continue holding up his hands. As a result, Joshua conquered the Amalekites.

What I love about this story is the recognition that it takes partnership, cooperation, and collaboration to gain the victory. It is not just Joshua or just Moses doing the work on their own—it is both of them, along with Aaron and Hur, who move immediately to help Moses when he is tired. This story is a picture of how we ought to function as a body in the church. It takes an entire team to win. We cannot overcome our battles alone. The moment individuals begin to gather to pray for a specific issue or carry a collective burden for a situation, the armies of the enemy will try to stop them at every turn, causing confusion, division, fatigue, rejection, or abandonment. But committed individuals who are gripped by the vision of prayer must carry out their corporate intercession regardless of the cost.

Unity is always the most important element. Without unity among a corporate body, the enemy of our souls can do some damage. As Watchman Nee rightly says, "Prayer is not the first thing to be done. Prayer only follows on the heels of harmony."[1] Every person must be of one accord. This is what Jesus meant when he said, "Again, truly I tell you that if two of you on earth agree about anything they ask for, it will be done for them by my Father in heaven" (Matthew 18:19). Agreement in spirit for God to move and work out his plan ought to be

---

1. Watchman Nee, *The Prayer Ministry of the Church: God Does Not Work Alone* (New York: Christian Fellow Publishers, Inc., 1973), 26.

our sole focus, but since we are human and bring context and perspectives to the table, we must be aware that the first thing the enemy will try to distort and destroy is the unity among God's people. Therefore, relinquishing control, surrendering competition, and submitting to proper authority ought always be present ingredients in the equation of prayer. Certainly, prayer meetings should be the driving force of the church since prayer is a ministry the church has practiced communally since its inception, when the disciples "devoted themselves . . . to prayer" (Acts 2:42). Although there is no *wrong* way to pray to the God of the universe, there are better ways than others, as well as certain cautions to be mindful of.

Considerations for Better Prayer Practices

First and foremost, prayer ought to be directed toward God on behalf of needs and individuals and never directed to anything or anyone else, which would be idolatry. The impact of globalization, the rise and spread of Eastern spirituality, the emergence of the New Age movement, and the influence of folk religions have made it easy for Christians to confuse prayer directed to the almighty God with mantras, methods, and meditations. While these things may be useful and have their own place in the life of someone who strives to love God and love others well, Christians ought to recognize and remember that we do not pray or bow to acknowledge any higher power other than God. We might use mantras or meditative routines to remind *ourselves* of what God's intentions for us are, but we do not use them to replace an intimate, dialogic prayer life between ourselves and God.

Second, our prayers should not seek to manipulate outcomes or events. I have seen some intercessors in their zeal begin to cry out asking God to intervene in particular situations, and in their passion they go into what many have called "commanding" prayers. They may begin to command the enemy to retreat, or command God to open the gates of heaven and take authority over things that are not theirs to direct. We Christians have authority over certain things—but not over the outcome of events. Therefore, our prayers ought always reflect surrender first, to the will of God and no other. In a prayer group once, I heard a lady praying for her daughter who had been gripped by a grueling alcohol addiction, asking God to make her so sick she would not be able to drink anymore. Although this woman's intent for the end goal—her daughter's deliverance from addiction—was good, her presumption to direct the manner by which this deliverance came was not right. We can pray for the deliverance, healing, and freedom of individuals without presuming to choose the manner in which it happens. Part of trusting that God will answer our prayers is that we leave it up to him to choose how. It is good and right to pray for the well-being of others.

Finally, I have heard many people give thanks for bad things that happen. In a prayer circle at a local church once, I heard several individuals give thanks for COVID. Although I am sure what they meant was not that they were grateful for the virus itself, which has killed millions around the world, but perhaps for some of its unanticipated results, such as more family time, appreciation for life, and a renewed awareness of the blessings we do have. Prayers like these could be harmful to anyone present who might have been devastated by COVID and saw none of the blessings that those lucky enough to escape the virus felt. Therefore, our prayers of gratitude should never be for what causes harm or evil but only for the good things and blessings that we experience. As the Word says, we are to "give thanks in all circumstances" (1 Thessalonians 5:18), not *for* all circumstances.

The Strength of Corporate Agreement

Watchman Nee says, "We need to realize that prayer is not just for personal use, nor is it only for devotional purpose. Prayer is a ministry, prayer is a work."[2] And this work ought to be the main focus and practice of Christians in order to recover the power of the Spirit. This power reenergizes and revives the body of Christ, propelling us forward with a new vigor to do

2. Nee, *The Prayer Ministry of the Church*, 27.

the greater works that Jesus promised we would do (see John 14:12). Corporate prayer prepares the way for God to move in unprecedented ways. We should never give up praying together, even when we might be weary or see little fruit, for at the right time the Lord will answer the prayers of his people.

Ultimately, programs and methods are human-centered and not Spirit-focused, so they can only do so much. Most of these efforts are inherently good, but they do not reach the depths of the human heart. Only the Spirit can do that, and the Spirit needs open vessels to work through and people who will gather to serve God's interests and not theirs; and God's interests are to reach the whole wide world and infuse all persons with his life-giving Spirit so they may come alive and be restored from their brokenness.

As the church begins to intercede, some practical reflections and implications are important to consider. First, individuals should take turns praying and refrain from praying more than twice in a single prayer meeting in order to give appropriate space for everyone to pray.

Second, it would be helpful to have a sense of guidance during the prayer so everyone knows what to pray for. One way that seems to create structure without too much formality is to pray for circles of influence: the inner circle, the outer circle, and the extended circle. The inner circle comprises the intercessors themselves, and the focus should be for unity among those who pray, for protection, guidance, and revelation for what to cover that day in the corporate session. Particularized personal situations should be covered in personal times of prayer or with a small group but not emphasized in the corporate prayer meeting. Corporate intercessory prayer focuses on the general interests of all. The outer circle are those in the church, in places of leadership, the pastoral team, children, and families of the community. The extended circle are the churches in the surrounding community, their pastors and families, community ministry partners and organizations, and any others in the community whom the church would seek to reach, such as those who do not know Jesus. God already has the desire to bless, redeem, and restore our civic communities, but he desires people to stand in the gap and pray that it may become a reality.

A unified church will be the collective effort of the righteous and the vehicle God uses to meet the needs of the world, creating an alternate consciousness that shapes the imagination of the faithful. In *Prayer Shield*, C. Peter Wagner offers some important insights as to why there is such a great need for intercessors to lift up their pastors and leaders in prayer: pastors have more responsibility and accountability, are more subject to temptation, are more targeted by spiritual warfare, have more influence on others, and have more visibility. Wagner elaborates on each topic, resulting in an excellent resource for Christian leaders. Wagner incites and invites Christians to be the shields of their pastors so they may do their work with joy and protection against the darts of the enemy. The most important indication of love and care for our leaders is measured in many ways, beginning with the commitment to and faithfulness in prayer.

In *Intercessory Prayer*, Dutch Sheets shares the story of Marlena, a lady who prayed for twelve years without any results for her brother to come to know Christ. Sheets says Marlena did not realize there were more specific ways to pray and proposes the following suggestions when praying for someone to come to a deeper knowledge of Christ:

- That God would lift the veil that covers the person
- For the Holy Spirit to hover over the individual and protect them
- For godly people to be in their pathway each day
- To cast down anything that would exalt itself against the knowledge of God, specifically pride and rebellion
- To take down all known strongholds: thought patterns, opinions on religion, materialism, and fear
- To bind Satan from taking the person captive, to bind all wicked thoughts and lies Satan would try to place in the mind
- That the armor of God would be placed on the person

Sheets mentions that, after two weeks of praying with these principles in mind, Marlena's brother overdosed on drugs and turned to God in his time of need.

Although Sheets offers great principles and suggestions to make our prayers more specific, his pragmatic perspective seems to indicate that the quick turn in this person's life came as a direct result of the use of these principles. Certainly, these principles might have helped Marlena formulate a better way to pray, but it does not prescribe a guaranteed outcome within a given timeframe. Some situations take years of consistent and constant intercession, regardless of the words we use. Nevertheless, praying such suggested words can help form a framework by which our prayer can be guided with the right motive, the right intention, and the right heart, and these are what God rewards.

A House of Prayer for all the Nations

Jesus entered the temple courts and drove out all who were buying and selling there. He overturned the tables of the money changers and the benches of those selling doves. "It is written," he said to them, "'My house will be called a house of prayer,' but you are making it 'a den of robbers.'" The blind and the lame came to him at the temple, and he healed them. But when the chief priests and the teachers of the law saw the wonderful things he did and the children shouting in the temple courts, "Hosanna to the Son of David," they were indignant.
—Matthew 21:12–15

Jesus made it clear that he desired the house of the Lord to be a house of prayer, but the religious people had turned it into a venue for private gain and economic pursuit. Jesus saw this occasion as an opportunity to overturn the *practices* of the religious leaders so that the *purpose* for the house of God could be reestablished. This purpose was twofold: (1) to purify the motives behind the practices of God's people and (2) to include those on the margins so they could come and find healing. While the religious leaders were consumed by greed, Jesus was consumed by zeal. In the Gospel of John, the author focuses on the zeal for God's house that consumed Jesus, making reference to Psalm 69:9: "For zeal for your house consumes me."

The zeal that consumed Jesus was nothing new. God himself had the same type of zeal, observable in the book of Haggai.

The Lord was distraught with the lack of concern and interest in building the house of the Lord while everyone was busy building their own: "Now this is what the LORD Almighty says: 'Give careful thought to your ways. You have planted much, but harvested little. You eat, but never have enough. You drink, but never have your fill. You put on clothes, but are not warm. You earn wages, only to put them in a purse with holes in it'" (1:5–6). God confronted the constant activity that consumed the people of God, challenging their motives and behaviors so they would turn their efforts to building his temple.

On the other hand, the synoptic Gospels (Matthew, Mark, and Luke) testify to Jesus's concern for inclusion and the healing of the "nations" (all peoples) instead of focusing on the purification of the temple. These accounts reveal the purposeful actions that would follow the purification of the temple. The concern does not seem to be with the *purification* of a space as much as with the *preparation* of the space so that those on the outside may benefit from what is taking place inside. Matthew specifically describes at length why Jesus's zeal consumed him, referencing Isaiah 56:6–7:

> And foreigners who bind themselves to the LORD to minister to him, to love the name of the LORD, and to be his servants, all who keep the Sabbath without desecrating it and who hold fast to my covenant—these I will bring to my holy mountain and give them joy in my house of

prayer. Their burnt offerings and sacrifices will be accepted on my altar; for my house will be called a house of prayer for all nations.

Isaiah not only declares that the house of the Lord is to be a house of prayer, but he also mentions that the goal is for those who have been excluded to be brought to the holy mountain to experience joy. The means by which this happens is through the repurposing of the house of the Lord so that outsiders may be brought in. Isaiah named two groups who were rejected by the law of Moses and the people of God: eunuchs (v. 4) and immigrants (v. 6). The law of Moses exiled both these groups from the people of Israel, but Isaiah urged them not to see themselves as excluded from the circle of faith and promised that they too belonged to the family of God. This prophetic understanding was controversial because eunuchs and immigrants were gentiles and did not belong to the nation of Israel, the chosen people of God. Nevertheless, it foreshadows the inclusion that Christ would proclaim and that the early Christian church took seriously.

In the Gospels it is evident that Jesus was consumed by his zeal for the house of the Lord so that God's people would be cleansed, purified, and sanctified. He also desired that those in the margins who had been excluded by the people of God would be included in the fellowship and find healing and joy in the house of prayer. In fact, we see this desire clearly when

Matthew describes the blind and the lame—previously excluded from worshiping inside the temple based on their physical deficiencies—were welcomed and healed by Jesus in the temple (21:14). After the healings took place, the children began shouting as a display of exuberant joy, and their shouts of acclamation were accepted as a pleasing offering and sacrifice of praise to Jesus.

This demonstration of praise caused the religious leaders a certain amount of indignation and consternation for a variety of reasons. It is possible they were jealous because the wonderful signs Jesus was performing competed with the market-oriented philosophy they held. They may also have been struggling with their interpretations of the law and holiness as compared to Jesus, whom they viewed as an unholy lawbreaker profaning their sacred temple space. Finally, they seemed upset that children were making noise, calling Jesus the Son of David—a holy title and a serious claim—and that nothing was being done to stop them. In the eyes of the religious leaders, Jesus profaned the holiness of the temple grounds by welcoming the least of these, accepting them, and healing those who had been excluded in order to fulfill the purpose for which he had been sent. Jesus was also paving the way to show his disciples how the movement of the church would be initiated: as a gathering of believers devoted to prayer who would be cleansed, filled, and empowered to reach out to all people in all nations—which is precisely what took place in Acts 2.

All the disciples and many of the women followers "joined together constantly in prayer" (Acts 1:14). Further, "When the day of Pentecost came, they were all together in one place. Suddenly a sound like the blowing of a violent wind came from heaven and filled the whole house where they were sitting" (2:1–2). Although it is unclear as to who was "all together" in this place when the Spirit descended, what *is* clear is that the in-breaking of the manifest presence of God in this place had important repercussions and effects. First, "all of them were filled with the Holy Spirit" (2:4), implying that the human spirit was now under the control of the Holy Spirit. Second, they began to speak in other languages—presumably languages they had not previously learned, which was a miracle in and of itself (v. 4). Finally, this occurrence drew many other faithful Jewish people to the house as they heard the Spirit-filled disciples speaking in their own various languages. All these people—from different regions far and wide, with different customs, cultures, and languages—were drawn to this house in bewilderment because each heard their own language being spoken (vv. 5–11). Acts 2 estimates that three thousand "were added to their number that day" (v. 41).

Practical Implications for the Ministry of Corporate Prayer

The existence of the house of prayer for the purpose of benefiting and blessing all nations is emphasized clearly in the story of the primitive church. When the disciples constantly met together to pray, they left room for the Holy Spirit to fill, empower, purify, sanctify, and bestow supernatural gifts for the equipping of the body. When meeting together as a church, the first objective ought to be one of *preparation* of the heart and the physical space to allow the Holy Spirit to move in ways that produce fruit beyond measure. A second objective of corporate prayers ought to be one of *separation* of resources, callings, and abilities to draw others to the love of God. A final objective must be one of *integration* of the different aspects of discipleship. Acts 2:42 lists several aspects of discipleship: being devoted to the apostolic teachings, fellowship, the breaking of bread, and prayer. Prayer perhaps served as the propelling force behind their endeavors and contributed to a sense of unity in their spirit, but it was not the only important aspect. Fellowship, strong teaching, and communion with one another were also important elements in the house of prayer.

Thus, the ministry of corporate prayer today ought to focus on these three objectives in order to remain faithful to the biblical vision. In the initiation of the church, we clearly see that the disciples remained faithful and active while also

133

leaving room for the Holy Spirit to do the unique saving of souls that only the Spirit can do. Rather than offering attractive programs, building appealing structures, or participating in disjointed benevolent efforts, the church today must rediscover the purpose for which it has been called into existence: to become a house of prayer for the benefit of all the nations. Instead of charting institutional health through quantifiable metrics, the church must be liberated to redefine its success through a prophetic imagination of what it would look like to have the kingdom in our midst. The kingdom with us is partly possible through the church's unwavering commitment to corporate prayer.

The preaching of the Word in a prayerless congregation will fall, lifeless and powerless, in front of the preacher. There will be no conduit to carry its power into the hearts of women and men because the atmosphere is cold and unfavorable. E. M. Bounds says it this way, "Just as some prayers never go above the head of him who prays, so the preaching of some preachers goes no farther than the front of the pulpit from which it is delivered. It takes prayer in the pulpit and prayer in the pew to make preaching arresting, life-giving, and soul-saving."[3] The preaching of the Word is interconnected with prayer. They are like twin towers. The more we pray, the more clear the Word

---

3. E. M. Bounds, *The Weapon of Prayer* (Grand Rapids: Baker Book House, 2004), 118–19.

becomes, almost as if it illuminates its pages so that it nourishes the preacher first and then the congregation. For that reason, corporate prayer ought to function as a symbiotic relationship, where the nourishment that is available through the Word of God becomes its natural result.

PART III

LISTENING PRAYER

"Spiritual conviction might feel like ideation and action. . . . A person senses a new and profound ability to let go of conventional ideas, comfort with ambiguity or contradiction, a new capacity to question, openness to new paradigms, reliance more on imagination than logic, and, among others, willingness to experiment and tolerate failure."

—Gregg Chenoweth, *Everyday Discernment*

❋ ❋ ❋

"Does anybody hear the knock? Jesus is knocking, knocking, knocking. He comes to cities and knocks; many of them just say, 'Go on somewhere else,' and they miss the day of their visitation. He goes to the next city, and the next, looking for individuals hungry to be part of a prophetic revolution and an apostolic reformation."

—James W. Goll, *The Seer: The Prophetic Power of Visions, Dreams, and Open Heavens*

7 ❋ THE LANGUAGES OF GOD

When I was learning to speak English, colloquialisms and other forms of figurative speech presented particular difficulties to me, as is common with anyone learning a new language. I remember talking to someone who had asked me to do something but then said, "Never mind." At first I thought, *What does that mean? To never think about my thoughts? To disregard theirs?* When I used my dictionary to try to understand the phrase, I learned it simply meant to forget it. Later in my learning I came across several idiomatic expressions that, if translated literally into other languages, would be laughable. For instance, when someone says it is "raining cats and dogs," the first image a non-native English speaker might picture would seem ridiculous. How can rain produce cats and dogs? Then there are those expressions that are so common, native speakers never think twice about using them, like "test the water," "you know the drill," "up for grabs," and many others. Surely, every language has some expressions that are not meant to be taken literally but can be understood through a process of learning and discernment as to how they point to deeper meanings that reveal their intricate symbolism.

The same could be said about the way God speaks. God speaks in many different ways and uses a variety of modes to communicate with his people. This chapter addresses three ways that God speaks, with the intent that we may learn to hear his voice more clearly and follow his guidance more closely. Understanding the languages of God will help nourish a life of prayer that is richer, fuller, and centered on Christ. Without a doubt, God understands every human language, but the way he speaks to us can be categorized in terms of approaches rather than a linguistic arrangement of appropriate grammar and syntax. I have categorized the approaches God uses to communicate in three main ways: *written* language, *spoken* language, and *visual* language.

Written Language: The Scriptures

All Scripture is God-breathed and is useful for teaching, rebuking, correcting and training in righteousness, so that the servant of God may be thoroughly equipped for every good work.
—2 Timothy 3:16–17

Christianity worships a God who reveals himself, his will, and his plan. We see this action clearly demonstrated through the written Word. From beginning to end, we find a grand narrative showing us the continuous plan of salvation that God initiates to bring healing and redemption to creation. The

Word of God shapes an alternative consciousness and fuels a missional calling for the people of God, teaching us what we are to believe about God, his nature, his movement, and his plan. The Word of God shows us what our response should be as a result of standing in relationship with God. Scripture contains a rule of faith and obedience, and they walk hand in hand. Considering the Word of God as authoritative in our lives allows us to shape our identity in a way that is deeply rooted in Christ, which will inevitably affect the way we live in community with others.

The Scriptures were written over the course of several centuries, and Christians believe they are God-breathed—that is, inspired by the Spirit of God. Therefore, they are inerrant (without error) regarding everything that pertains to salvation, which is the central message of the Scriptures. The Spirit of God interacted with human writers who penned the words contained in the Bible. In the same way, the Spirit of God still interacts with the church, guiding us to discern how he speaks to humans as we read and interpret the Bible.

Interpreting the Bible is truly an art. It requires us to approach the text not as a science manual or a literary book but as the very words of God. God desires to reveal to us something about his character and purposes so that we may come to know him better and learn how to live a life worthy of him. For that reason, listening to the Word of God as we read it necessitates that we learn something about the text first and how to interpret what was written. Although it would be beyond the scope of this chapter to present a thorough description of how to read and interpret the text, I will share a few concise working principles that might be helpful in the process.

The Bible is available in many different translations. For the versions that have been translated into English, some aim to be closer to the original languages of Hebrew (Old Testament) and Greek (New Testament), such as the English Standard Version (ESV) and Revised Standard Version (RSV). Other translations paraphrase in an effort to reveal the intent of the text, such as The Message (MSG) or the New Living Translation (NLT). Yet others are somewhere in the middle, providing a dynamic equivalence in which the concept is retained as closely as possible even if the translation is not word for word, such as the New International Version (NIV).

Knowing the type of translation or the version being used is the first step to understanding and faithful interpretation. Second, the text must be read in its context rather than picking and choosing individual verses. Although at times God may clearly speak to us through one particular verse, that verse is surrounded by a host of other verses for a reason. Finally, difficult and obscure passages must be understood in light of the clear overarching message inside the book itself.

Each book in the Bible was written to a particular audience at a particular time in history, and each book also has a specific genre. Therefore, the Bible should not be read or interpreted literally. For example, Matthew records in two different passages some pretty striking words that Jesus says to his disciples: "If your right eye causes you to stumble, gouge it out and throw it away. It is better for you to lose one part of your body than for your whole body to be thrown into hell" (5:29). "And if your eye causes you to stumble, gouge it out and throw it away. It is better for your to enter life with one eye than to have two eyes and be thrown into the fire of hell" (18:9). This topic must have been pretty important to Jesus if he addressed it twice. Although these words are strong, Jesus does not mean them literally. What Jesus means is that if we recognize the tendency toward temptation in ourselves, we should do everything in our power to remove ourselves from situations that may tempt us. Jesus used hyperbole to demonstrate the severity of falling into continual patterns of temptation that would hinder us and possibly also cause others to stumble. Nevertheless, it would be incongruent with Jesus's own actions to think he would want his people to harm ourselves. Jesus not only healed many blind people and restored their sight, but he also saw the eye as something good: "But blessed are your eyes because they see, and your ears because they hear" (Matthew 13:16). Thus, learning to hear the voice of God in the Bible requires us to learn to understand the individual particularities in light of the whole.

Another important aspect of learning to hear the voice of God is recognizing the different types of texts we may encounter. There are *normative* texts, which are universal teachings for everyone, such as the greatest commandments (to love God and love our neighbors) and the Great Commission (to make disciples of all nations). There are other passages that are *descriptive*, telling us what happened in the story. And there are still more passages that are *corrective*, seeking to address specific issues. A lot of the Pauline letters are corrective because Paul wrote to deal with concerns that arose in the various churches he planted and mentored. Paul's writings should be read within their historical and literary contexts first, and applied to our lives in the contemporary world second.

Seeking understanding of the Word of God implies knowing how to read the Word of God, which will help prepare us to meet the Spirit of God as we read. God speaks to us through the written Word, and meditating on it day and night will make the reader like a tree planted by streams of water that become refreshing to the soul (see Psalm 1).

Spoken Language: *Rhema*

As we read the words of God carefully in the Scriptures, our endeavor becomes preparatory in a sense. It prepares us to encounter the Spirit of God through his *rhema*. *Rhema* is a Greek word that appears seventy-three times in the New Testament and refers to the spoken word, or utterance, that is fresh and active and helps us in our times of need. There are two Greek words often translated as "word": *logos* and *rhema*. With the notable exception of when the Gospel of John uses it to describe Jesus, *logos* usually refers to the logical arrangement of the parts of speech, while *rhema* involves a more interactive and dynamic exchange, denoting something that is being stated expressly for its application in a particular scenario.

For example, I will never forget the story of a young girl who was going through a dire time. She found herself in the middle of a bridge contemplating ending her suffering. She hadn't attended church since she was a kid. But all of a sudden the words she had learned during a particular Vacation Bible School summer came into her mind: "Be still and know that I am God." This *rhema*—the living and active utterance that came into her thoughts—altered her emotions to the extent that she changed her mind and decided she wanted to live. Later she testified that the Word of God literally saved her life. Thus, *rhema* refers to God's intentional revelation when the Holy Spirit speaks to individuals.

The significance of *rhema* is exemplified in the instruction to "take the sword of the Spirit, which is the word [*rhema*] of God" (Ephesians 6:17). Here the reference is not to the entire narrative of the Scriptures as a whole but to the individual passages or utterances that might be spoken by the Spirit to help us in our time of need. When Jesus faced his temptation in the desert, he said, "It is written: 'Man shall not live on bread alone, but on every word [*rhema*] that comes from the mouth of God'" (Matthew 4:4). In other words, our daily sustenance comes from nourishing our bodies *and* nourishing our spirit. We should certainly nourish our minds as well through an educated process of learning how to read and interpret the *written* word of God (*logos*). But when it comes to nourishing the spirit, the Word must become alive and activate something within us that is fresh, new, and applicable for our lives—which is where *rhema* becomes important. Depending on our life's circumstances, the Spirit of God may speak to us through different passages, verses, promises, or utterances that are individualized to produce in us the type of encouragement, resilience, inspiration, motivation, or aid that is needed to overcome our present difficulties or maintain the vitality of our Christian faith.

Sometimes God's *rhema* is offered through other individuals, like pastors, mentors, accountability partners, or small groups. This type of *rhema* is often called "prophetic language," which means it serves to encourage or console or challenge others. Paul offers an example in 1 Corinthians 14:3: "But the one who prophesies speaks to people for their strengthening, encouraging and comfort." These prophetic words must be practiced with great care, recognizing that we only see and prophesy in part (1 Corinthians 13:9, 12), so our attempt to encourage others and console them through God's *rhema* is incomplete, temporary, and symbolic at best. Only the Spirit of God can produce the type of encouragement, strengthening, and consolation that each person needs to maintain a vigorous faith. Nevertheless, *rhema* given by other people should serve to confirm direction and provide guidance to the recipient. I have received many prophetic words from others. Some have come to pass, others haven't yet, and still others I have rejected because they had no scriptural basis or were founded on speculative nonsense. *Rhema* offered by others should not be taken literally but should always be subjected to a process of validation, which is possible only through the confirmation of mature believers and the revelation of the written Word of God.

It would be incomplete to conclude this section without talking about *rhema* as revelation. It is not just an utterance, prophetic word, or spoken words. It is the revelation of Christ himself. Even though Christ is often called the *Logos* of God (John 1 and 1 John 1), he is associated with *rhema* in Luke 2:15: "When the angels had left them and gone into heaven, the shepherds said to one another, 'Let's go to Bethlehem and see this thing [*rhema*] that has happened, which the Lord has told us about.'" The baby—the Savior the angels announced—was the revelation, the word of God that came to be just as it was spoken. Apart from the incarnation, death, and resurrection of Christ, we would only have an incomplete understanding of how God speaks and a partial vision of how he reveals his nature, purposes, and plans. Through the Christ event we see the extent of God's love for humanity.

Visual Language: Dreams and Visions

Now we have come to the final section, sometimes referred to as dark speeches or riddles because of their inherent symbolism and difficulty to comprehend at face value. Why would God choose to speak obscurely and not plainly? Perhaps because God wants us to be attentive in our discernment. Jesus did not always speak plainly. He spoke in parables and using figurative language so that those who were really determined to follow him would be diligent enough to seek understanding. In the same way, God speaks symbolically and figuratively through imagery, dreams, and visions.

Because in the West we have been largely influenced by Aristotelian philosophy, which affirms that knowledge can only be acquired through sense and reason, we tend to dismiss any other source of potential knowledge as superstition or mysticism. In the Bible, however, we see God often speaking to individuals through dreams and visions. Therefore, it is important to consider this type of language as a valid way God communicates with his people. In the book of Job we learn how God uses dreams to speak: "For God does speak—now one way, now another—though no one perceives it. In a dream, in a vision of the night, when deep sleep falls on people as they slumber in their beds, he may speak in their ears and terrify them with warnings, to turn them from wrongdoing and keep them from pride, to preserve them from the pit, their lives from perishing by the sword" (33:14–18). According to this passage, God uses dreams to offer wisdom and instruction, to produce a change in perspective, to warn of possible dangers, and to keep us from falling into traps. We find God using dreams for these purposes throughout the Bible.

Visions and dreams come from the deepest level of the psyche. The next chapter will present more fully how to interpret these experiences by learning to discern their source since they do not always come as a result of revelation, but sometimes as an indication of unresolved conflicts that are suppressed in the subconscious or as provocative imaginations connected to something we might have been deeply considering during the day or night before. In this chapter, however, the intent is to present biblical examples that shed light on and give witness to the manner in which God has often chosen to communicate with his people through dreams and visions in order to reveal something about the future, symbolically and purposefully.

Let's consider Abraham first. Genesis 15:1 says, "The word of the LORD came to Abram in a vision: 'Do not be afraid,

Abram. I am your shield, your very great reward.'" The vision contained images as well as sounds and was very personal, coming as a sign of encouragement and strengthening his faith. Later that evening, "Abram fell into a deep sleep, and a thick and dreadful darkness came over him" (v. 12). Then we read that the Lord spoke to him while he slept (v. 13). The darkness was symbolic in and of itself, providing context for the dream. The dream was a sign of what was to come to Abraham's descendants, who would be mistreated and enslaved in a country not their own (v. 13).

Then there was Joseph, the dreamer, who saw through symbols what would take place later in his life, even when he did not understand the meaning at the time (see Genesis 37). When Joseph found himself in prison for something he hadn't done, he met a cupbearer and a baker who also had dreams. Joseph interpreted their dreams for them in ways that came to pass just as he said (see Genesis 40). The same happened with Pharaoh, who dreamed concerning his land in Egypt, and Joseph was also able to interpret his dreams (see Genesis 41). Dreams should not be interpreted literally but, with discernment, can be understood as symbols for and representations of other things.

Like Joseph, Daniel was also prepared to understand and interpret dreams. Daniel shows us the value of warning, instruction, wisdom, and new perspectives that are possible by carefully tuning in to how God speaks to us in the night. For instance, what is clearly seen in the nighttime conversation God has with Nebuchadnezzar are two principles that help us understand the role of dreams and visions. Daniel says Nebuchadnezzar's dreams showed two things in particular: the thoughts of his heart and mind and the outcome of his decisions if he continued on the path he was going (Daniel 2:29–30).

In the New Testament we find God continuing to speak through dreams. Consider Joseph, engaged to Mary, being told that Mary's baby was God's Son and should be named Jesus (Matthew 1:20–21). Later, Joseph was warned in a dream to take Jesus and Mary and flee to Egypt (2:13). In yet another dream years later, Joseph received confirmation and detailed instruction concerning his family's safety after Herod's death (2:19–20). Wise men were also warned in a dream to avoid Herod, so they returned home by a different route (2:12).

Dreams may offer warning or instruction from God to alert us to potential dangers along our path or guide our decision-making. However, not all dreams are from God. Dreams may reveal the depth of our unconscious realities that often get suppressed and come to the surface at night, revealing our fears, concerns, or unresolved conflicts in the psyche. In the next chapter, I will describe several principles of interpretation that can help guide the process of discernment. Here, I share an example to show that not all dreams are signs from God, especially if they are recurring nightmares, which may indicate psychological stress or trauma related to a past event. We know that, while God may encourage us out of our comfort zones in order to step into the mission and calling he has for us, God does not rule us by fear and manipulation.

A friend of mine came to me one day to share a recurring dream her child was having. In this dream the child kept falling into lava and drowning, causing him to wake up crying from fright. I explained to her that psychological science has determined that recurring nightmares often indicate a type of suppressed fear and are not necessarily divine warnings or revelatory. This child's subconscious had probably filtered a negative experience, and I suggested that my friend train her child to get inside his dream the next time it happened and intentionally see himself coming back out from the lava rather than drowning. The child needed help seeing himself as an overcomer in order to stop the nightmare's recurring effect so that his mind would learn to deal with the fear at its source. I received a message from the mother a few months later saying he told her that, when he had the same dream again, he saw himself coming out of the lava, protected by his gear and totally unharmed. Several years later I asked her how he was doing, and she told me he had never reported having that dream again.

Visions—which come to an awake, conscious person as opposed to dreams, which come to a sleeping person—also serve several purposes in the Bible: to strengthen faith, to share a promise, to confirm direction, provide guidance, and to make a revelation. Let's consider some examples in the New Testament. When Saul found himself making threats against the early church, he was met with a bright light on the road to Damascus. As he fell to the ground, he heard the voice of the Lord speaking to him, and after the vision was over, Saul found himself unable to see anything (see Acts 9:1–9). Meanwhile, the Lord called Ananias through a vision to visit Saul and lay his hands on him so his eyesight could be restored (see Acts 9:10–19).

Visions transcend our human capacities and give indication of a type of communication that is available through the gifts of God. In the beginning of Acts, we find Peter witnessing to this fact when he makes reference to a prophecy in the Old Testament, which says that in the last days God would pour out his Spirit on all people and his sons and daughters would prophesy while the young men would see visions and the old men would dream dreams (Acts 2:17).

Cornelius, a centurion and devout man, also had a vision one day, receiving instruction and guidance (Acts 10). Peter had a vision while he was in a trance (Acts 10:9–16). A trance is a half-conscious state characterized by an absence of response to external stimuli. In Acts 10, Peter's trance led to a vision, which led him to accept those in Cornelius's house who professed to believe in Jesus, even though they were not Jewish. Peter's vision and his response to it paved the way for the first solution to the problem of integration in the Christian church as gentiles came to know Christ. Through his vision, Peter allowed God to confront Peter's own prejudice against the gentiles in the form of amending Jewish regulations regarding unclean animals.

Paul had a vision during one of his missionary journeys about a Macedonian man pleading with Paul to come and help. Paul left for Macedonia at once, trusting it was God giving guidance and confirming the next step in his journey (see Acts 16:6–10).

The revelation of Jesus concerning the future was given personally to John through many symbols, figures, or images (see the book of Revelation).

Dreams and visions are God's symbolic and visual language that contains images, utterances, and pictures to serve as signs, provide confirmation, or offer guidance. One of the most common errors is to interpret dreams and visions literally, which is the topic of the next chapter.

8 ❋ DISCERNING THE VOICE OF GOD

The Western world has been permeated by rationalism, which has left us suspicious of potential supernatural activity. The rationalism so prevalent in our society today was largely influenced by the Enlightenment period as well as Aristotelian philosophy and Freudian psychology, all of which affirm reason as the highest virtue. These ideologies tell us not to attend to any voices other than the voice of reason. But we hear voices in our head all the time that may or may not be considered logical. Of course, some individuals hear them in an unbalanced way, which may cause them to do destructive things. Nevertheless, we are all aware that each of us harbors a plethora of competing voices, some that are constructive and helpful and others that bind us in cycles of self-defeat. We hear the voices of our own desires, the voice of conscience, the voice of public opinion, the voice of temptation, the voice of accusation, the voice of common sense, the voice of worry—and so on. Those voices are internal, and we must learn to distinguish and then address their sources. It is important for us to learn to discern which voices are worth heeding and which should be ignored or quieted so we may also learn to recognize the voice of God.

The Voices We Hear

Identifying the source of the voices we hear is the way to create a path of discernment, which is necessary in order to learn to recognize God's voice. First, there are the sensory voices, which come from the five senses as we see, hear, smell, taste, and touch. These sensory inputs provide a basis of knowledge, and we absorb the messages that come from these senses. Learning to filter the information we receive is important because it has the potential to distort our self-perception or the perception of others and make us less prone to hear the voice of God.

Second, there are the voices that stem from our own reasoning, logic, and common sense. For example, it makes sense to take a shower after we have done a workout, so the voice of reason invites and compels us to engage in such, but there are other times we might prefer to go to bed dirty because the voice of emotion may win over the voice of reason. God sometimes will speak to us through the voice of reason, just like he warned Israel by reminding them of what happened to them when they ignored the laws of God (see Deuteronomy

8:11–20). God expects us to use our minds to work through possible solutions based on reason.

A third source is emotion, which often speaks loudly and compellingly. We feel exhausted. We groan or despair. We give in to fear, anger, or anxiety. The voice of emotion often exclaims and signals that something in the environment or the past is triggering a response internally. Listening to that voice is important to validate our feelings and secure a way forward. The emotional side may also spur us to acts of compassion or service. Just like Jesus had compassion for the multitudes that were hungry (Matthew 14, 15; Mark 6, 8; Luke 9; John 6), the voice of his compassion in us might motivate us.

Fourth is the voice of conscience. Conscience is an inner voice that serves as a compass and guide for our morality and behavior. We experience pangs of conscience as a result of our failures or sins that keep guilt at the forefront of our minds. A troubled conscience is often the result of an inability to remedy the past and an insatiable desire for homeostasis in the future. Although we know "there is now no condemnation for those who are in Christ Jesus" (Romans 8:1), those who are gripped by the pangs of conscience over past, forgiven transgressions must learn to defeat that voice by providing an alternative that counteracts its effects. Humor is an effective approach. Comedic forms have long been employed to liberate the dominating and gravitational forces that pull the self toward an archaic and deplorable state. Performing extreme acts of penance or inflicting self-harm as an attempt to alleviate a conscience often represents false humility or yields shallow results.

Fifth is the voice of authority figures, like parents, teachers, pastors, mentors, and leaders, influencing us to make certain kinds of choices and decisions. Their voices can affect us, consciously or unconsciously, positively or negatively. God can use the voices of authority figures as if they were his voice to us to influence us for good. Conversely, the voices of authority figures can be misdirected and become the voice of the enemy. At times, we are the authority figures, holding a type of power over others. The words we use to speak to those under us have an important impact on their self-perception and life trajectory. Therefore, we should always be careful with the words we use.

Finally, the voice of the enemy needs to be accounted for. Interestingly enough, he may use our senses as his means of communication. He also may use reason as the battlefield where he can deceive, planting doubt and distrust in our minds so we question God's word and revelation. He can also use our emotions as his playground, sowing despair and discouragement along the way so we give up pursuing God. He can use our conscience, and when the conscience is wrongly trained, it can easily become the voice of accusation, judgment, or prejudice. He may also empower and energize someone in authority, even in a ministry position, to misuse their power and inflict pain or cause harm through their selfish decisions.

How can we discern the voice of God in the midst of so many other voices?

Recognizing God's Voice

God speaks directly to our spirit. Our spirits are quickened the moment we are born into the kingdom of heaven. The voice of God is most clearly heard and discerned through the community of faith. Nevertheless, we can be taught directly by the Spirit of God according to our spiritual giftings. Paul was taught by the Spirit: "These are the things God has revealed to us by his Spirit. The Spirit searches all things, even the deep things of God. For who knows a person's thoughts except their own spirit within them? . . . The person without the Spirit does not accept the things that come from the Spirit of God but considers them foolishness, and cannot understand them because they are discerned only through the Spirit" (1 Corinthians 2:10–11, 14). It is neither improbable nor impossible for a person who has not been rebirthed into the kingdom of God to hear the voice of God in its many inflections, although it is not likely that the individual will understand or discern it apart from the body of Christ.

Throughout Scripture, God spoke to many people in different ways. God spoke to Elijah not through a powerful wind, a great earthquake, or a fire but through a gentle whisper (1 Kings 19). His gentle whisper guides us when stressful events tempt us to despair. But God does not always or exclusively use a gentle whisper. Sometimes he does use a powerful wind, as when he showed up when all the believers were gathered in one place on Pentecost (Acts 2). God spoke to Moses through a bush that kept burning (Exodus 3) and to Samuel through a voice in the middle of the night (1 Samuel 3). God answered Paul and Silas's prayers through a violent earthquake that shook the foundations of the prison where they had been put, and everyone's chains came loose (Acts 16).

God does indeed speak differently and uses different means by which to reveal his power and presence. He is not bound by time or spatial categories—God is creative! God is infinite, immortal, invisible, and beyond our human capacity to comprehend him. Paul affirms these truths when he says, "However, as it is written: 'What no eye has seen, what no ear has heard, and what no human mind has conceived'—the things God has prepared for those who love him—these are the things God has revealed to us by his Spirit" (1 Corinthians 2:9–10). Our minds are not able to conceive what is in the spiritual realm unless it is revealed by the Spirit. The revelation of the Spirit assures us that we are children of God and that no one can pluck us from his hands (John 10:29). God may illuminate our minds so our thought patterns are renewed, and he can stabilize our emotions. Our bodies feel the effects of the soul (emotions, thoughts, decision-making).

God may also speak through our experiences. In his book *Everyday Discernment,* Gregg Chenoweth presents three types of guidance we might encounter by examining Paul's experiences. Type I refers to those experiences initiated by God to provide guidance and direction. Examples are the occurrences on Paul's journeys: miracles, visions, and supernatural interventions like healings and earthquakes. Type II are those experiences given by God inside the community, such as when a group of people appointed Paul after prayer to be commissioned. Type III pertains to naturally occurring events that offered supernatural insight. For example, a belt symbolized for Paul what would be coming to him (imprisonment) later in his journey.[1]

Jesus says his followers know and abide by his voice and not the voice of a stranger. But in today's world—with rapidly changing technology, the rise of globalization, and the levels of brokenness that are damaging our souls—it can be difficult to hear and be guided by the voice of Jesus alone. I remember talking to a young man who said he was driving his car one day and heard what he thought was God telling him to close his eyes while he was driving if he really trusted God. So he did.

---

1. Gregg Chenoweth, *Everyday Discernment: The Art of Cultivating Spirit-Led Leadership* (Kansas City, MO: The Foundry Publishing, 2021), 26.

As you might imagine, he ended up in an accident and was referred to a psychiatrist, who diagnosed him as schizophrenic. The young man was confused, shocked, and alarmed, not knowing anymore what to do or whom to trust. I assured him he was not schizophrenic and told him that he had probably heard the voice of the enemy, who wanted to destroy him. I suggested that he learn to use the voice of reason and common sense to counteract the enemy's voice, since God would never ask us to put ourselves in danger just to show we trusted him. In fact, this is exactly how the devil tempted Jesus in the wilderness when he said Jesus should throw himself from the highest point of the temple and trust that God's angels would protect him (Luke 4:9). Jesus resisted him by reasoning that God should not be put to the test (v. 12).

This young man's story does not mean that mental illness is always an incorrect diagnosis. Listening to the voice of experts can be a way to allow reason to confirm what we might be experiencing in real life. Because we all hear conflicting voices at times, these voices need to be tested and confirmed, accounting for human error—because we do not always hear correctly.

Testing and Confirming the Source

There are several ways to test and confirm the voice of God since we know the enemy can counterfeit experiences and distort our perception. Thus, we learn to interpret experiential types of guidance that come through revelatory means by aligning our experiences with Scripture, reason, tradition, prayer, and the confirmation or perspective of mature believers. When my husband, Andrew, was going through medical treatments, we visited many healing and prayer conferences. At some of these conferences people were enthusiastic and hopeful and came to pray over him, often proclaiming their confidence that Andrew would be healed. But these words were premature and came from a strong desire and influence of their own thinking rather than revelation from God. Paul says we know in part and prophesy in part, but when perfection comes the imperfect disappears (see 1 Corinthians 13:9-10). For that reason, prophetic words need to be confirmed by other words, including the Word of God.

Sometimes our own feelings can indicate something about how God speaks. Perhaps you are feeling weighed down and heavy, so you ask yourself, *Where is this heaviness in my spirit coming from? Is it my sin? The toxicity and stress of my current environment? Could it be the enemy using certain compulsions to gain ground and bring me down?* Recognizing the source of our feelings can help us ascertain how God is speaking to our spirit. Then, if we release whatever is causing us strain, we may walk in the power of the Spirit and in the freedom, joy, peace, and love God has for us. As another example, perhaps we might have a strong sensitivity to the feelings of other people and want to show compassion or create harmony. It is commendable to bear each other's burdens, but only to a point. God does not want us to be so weighed down that we are crushed and hindered from walking in freedom. We must learn to bear the burdens of others through prayer and, when we feel released, leave them at the foot of the cross and rest in the promise that God has it.

We know God can speak through dreams, but not all dreams come from God. One way to discern the source is to evaluate its *effect*. Learning to discern his guidance through dreams has required me to gain a level of expertise in the subject matter so I can truly know whether the dream is from God. For example, about a year after my husband's passing, I had a disconcerting dream and woke up alarmed. In this dream I saw myself walking down the stairs, going to meet my husband. All of a sudden, I could no longer move or speak, so Andrew started to walk upstairs to help me. Just then, he received a shot in his head. He started bleeding and could not move either. Suddenly I became mobile again and began to knock on the walls frantically, calling for help, but my sister-in-law, who was doing dishes in the kitchen, could not hear me. Then I woke up crying and wondering, *What is God trying to say to me?* Or was the dream revealing some internal unresolved trauma that the devil was using to make me afraid and anxious?

Interestingly, that morning my young son, Lucas, told me he had had the most amazing dream that same night. He shared that he was walking with his uncle (the husband of the sister-in-law who had appeared in my dream), and they were shooting bows and arrows. When Lucas shot the target, the arrow pierced it with such might that the target opened, and he described seeing a stairway to heaven where his daddy was next to Jesus. I did not tell Lucas about my own dream, of course, but his dream was God's assurance to me that, although the enemy had tried to bring fear and anxiety through my dream, Lucas's dream was God's way of bringing peace, joy, and assurance.

There have been other instances when dreams have been revelatory and served as warnings to guide my path and help me know what decisions to make in uncertain times, as well as promises of breakthroughs God would bring in the future.

One key for discerning the source of a revelation is learning to distinguish acts of God from acts of other spiritual forces. There is always the potential for misinterpretation as well as fraud and false prophecy. The Scriptures testify to the way hostile powers can imitate divinity, such as with Pharaoh's magicians (Exodus 7); Elymas/Bar-Jesus (Acts 13); or Simon the sorcerer (Acts 8). Scripture also describes the way false prophets worked signs (Matthew 24:24; Mark 13:22; 2 Thessalonians 2:9; Revelation 13:13). Craig Keener points out that spiritual leaders and prophets in ancient Israel often "prophesied blessings despite immorality, making up their own messages."[2] The prophet Jeremiah emphasized God's rejection of counterfeit prophets (23:11–30). We should remember that false prophets do not invalidate true prophets, whose obedience and righteous lives will testify to their authenticity. An easy way to distinguish whether the messenger or message is truly aligned with God is by their *fruit*. Another criterion is to be aware of whom the prophets are exalting—our Lord or themselves. The biblical record shows us multiple examples of false prophets, identifying them as those who call us to bow down to idols or other gods (Deuteronomy 13:1–5); those who deny Jesus as Messiah and draw attention to themselves instead (1 John 2:22); those who use grace as an excuse to continue sinning (Jude 1:4); and those who promote immorality (Revelation 2:14).

When a prophetic word is released it must be confirmed, either through Scripture or through other people. The predictive element of prophetic words should be treated as a caution rather than an unalterable foreshadowing. When more than one person offers the same or similar prophetic words, they might point to a specific calling or promise of God. Craig Keener offers an example from his own life. His wife grew up as a refugee in a country where few white people lived, yet

---

2. Craig S. Keener, *Miracles Today: The Supernatural Work of God in the Modern World* (Grand Rapids: Baker Academic, 2021), 238.

various individuals independently prophesied that she would marry a white minister. The prophecy had little chance of fulfillment, and the probability of coincidence was low. Yet the prophecy came to pass years later.[3]

Prophetic words must be tested, and sometimes it takes years for a prophetic word we receive to come to pass. A good example is Abram. God made his Word known to Abram and gave him a *promise*. Abram believed God against all odds, and it was "credited to him as righteousness" (Genesis 15:6). The Lord promised Abram that his descendants would be as numerous as the stars in the sky and assured him he would "take possession" of the land God showed him (v. 7).

Abram asked God how he could know God's promise was true (v. 8). God asked Abram to select a few animals as an offering (vv. 9–10). Abram brought them and arranged everything before God, but instead of God's presence showing up, the enemy showed up: "Then birds of prey came down on the carcasses, but Abram drove them away" (v. 11).

We will always have opposition and resistance from the evil one as he tries to stop us from obtaining the promises of God. But, like Abram, we can learn to drive away the interference of the evil one as we remain confident in God's promises. If we remain faithful in the process, God's purpose and plan

---

3. Keener, *Miracles: The Credibility of the New Testament Accounts,* Vol. 2 (Grand Rapids: Baker Academic, 2011), 882.

will not be thwarted. Abram teaches us that we must persist when the test comes: "Yet [Abraham] did not waver through unbelief regarding the promise of God, but was strengthened in his faith and gave glory to God, being fully persuaded that God had power to do what he had promised" (Romans 4:20–21). And, like Abram, we must persevere until God's promise is fulfilled in our lives.

Perseverance must be balanced with times of rest. We get a glimpse of this stage in what Abram did next. "As the sun was setting, Abram fell into a deep sleep, and a thick and dreadful darkness came over him" (Genesis 15:12). The process of obtaining the promises of God includes times of rest and purification. In the gloom of the night, the stars in the sky could no longer be counted. The sun was gone, and darkness had fallen. Any sign that pointed to the promise of God was now invisible. Right in the midst of incredible difficulty, God spoke to Abram about a wonderful future for both Abram and for God's people (vv. 15–16). Then, "when the sun had set and darkness had fallen, a smoking firepot with a blazing torch appeared and passed between the pieces" (v. 17). God showed up, making good on his promise. Likewise, we can rest assured that his Word can be trusted, even when it must be tested.

God: The Great Semiotician

Semiotics is the study of signs and their interpretations. It includes the analysis of symbols, metaphors, images, and pictures. Throughout the entire narrative of Scripture we find God speaking through signs. Signs reveal deeper meanings, and often those meanings have to be understood through patterns of interpretation. Although dream interpretation is often understood through the lenses of Jung or Freud and, more empirically, through neurologists, the prophetic role of dreams remains obscure and understudied. Historian Mark Knoll points out that Christians in Africa "are not surprised when Jesus speaks to them in dreams and visions."[4] Craig Keener asserts that "visions and dreams seem to proliferate particularly in times of spiritual intensity, for example, the Presbyterian revivals in the Hebrides in 1939."[5] Conversely, in times of spiritual apathy and stagnation, dreams and visions do not often appear, as was the case when "Samuel ministered before the LORD under Eli. In those days the word of the LORD was rare; there were not many visions" (1 Samuel 3:1).

One rule of thumb when trying to interpret dreams or visions is to do it retrospectively so we may interpret what we perceive in the spirit. We can distinguish revelatory dreams or

---

4. Mark Noll, *The New Shape of World Christianity: How American Experience Reflects Global Faith* (Downers Grove, IL: IVP Academic, 2009), 23–24.
5. Keener, *Miracles*, 877.

visions from inaccurate ones and make room for mistakes as we interpret them. A month after my husband was diagnosed with brain cancer, I began an intentional fast to seek the Lord's direction and intercede on Andrew's behalf. For three nights in a row, I was awakened at 4:00 a.m. to pray. As I prayed by my bedside, the Lord gave me visions each night. Here, I will only share the second vision the Lord gave me to show how we must make room for human error when interpreting signs from God. In the vision I saw a big boat, like a warship, navigating in the middle of a storm. Then I saw the engine and heard a voice that said, "Do you see the engine? These are the prayers of my people that will carry you." Then I saw Andrew, who was asleep in the bottom of the ship. I saw myself attending to him and running upstairs to the deck, where I would jump up and down and command those high, stormy waves to be still. Then I saw no more waves. The boat was engulfed by darkness. Then I saw a dove flying with a branch in its beak, coming toward me. The boat made it to the shore, and the sun began to shine, and I saw someone holding my hand.

For two and a half years, what I saw in this vision was mostly all I did. I attended to my husband at his sickbed and spent time every day commanding the waves to be still through prayer, praise, and daily intercession. I knew the vision was both symbolic and revelatory, and I assumed Andrew would be healed because I saw someone holding my hand. So I told everyone I knew to join with me in prayer and intercession because Andrew would be healed from terminal brain cancer. I proclaimed that, no matter how dark and difficult it got, he would make it out of the storm all right.

But he did not. Looking back, I see that the darkness that engulfed the boat represented his death, and the dove with a branch in its beak represented God's peace during that time of grief. The image at the end where we were holding hands simply meant Andrew's life would remain a source of strength and inspiration as I continued on the journey God had set for me.

Ever since that first time God showed me part of his plans through a series of visions, I began to dream frequently. Those dreams either came to pass immediately, or served as promises of what the Lord might want to do and reveal in the future. Here, I offer a few guidelines by which to interpret the symbolism of dreams based on personal experience and research. Among some of the most biblically sound resources are Herman Riffel's *Voice of God: The Significance of Dreams, Visions, and Revelations*; John Paul Jackson's *Top 20 Dreams*; and James Goll's *The Seer: The Prophetic Power of Visions, Dreams, and Open Heavens*. I recommend any of these for the reader who is interested in seeking a more robust understanding on this topic.

The purpose of understanding our dreams is to learn to recognize patterns or meanings that can be helpful as we are guided by the Spirit. By looking at what John Paul Jackson called "divine logic" in our dreams, we can begin to decipher the revelation of God, helping bridge our logic and his logic. Just like Jesus used parables, proverbs, stories, figurative speech, and metaphors, God also uses pictures and symbols to speak to us in the night. Similarities and differences must be filtered through three important factors: details in the dream, context of the dream, and present life circumstances. For example, I had a dream one night about my daughter, Sofia, who was three at the time. We were playing in a pool, and she was swimming, but I was carrying a heavy backpack full of books, and only my legs were submerged. All of a sudden, Sofia began to drown. I got closer to her, but I could not move fast because my backpack was very heavy, so I threw it in the water and swam to rescue her. When I got her out of the water, her eyes were open and she was fine.

Rather than taking this dream literally and waking up alarmed, I knew it signaled something else. The details and the context of the dream provided enough information for me to understand how to apply it and what God was revealing to me about my daughter. My backpack full of books represented my work because I live in the world of academia, and the pool represented Sofia's world of play. She was playing all alone while I was busy with my work. When I recognized that she was drowning in her loneliness, I sensed God telling me to lay down my work and give more attention and time to my daughter. That same day I left work early, picked up my children from school, and took them to the children's museum. In fact, I decided that everything else could go on the back burner for a while, and I was more intentional about spending time every afternoon and evening with my kids, especially Sofia. The details of a dream must be understood in light of their symbolism and not taken literally. I could have woken up from that dream terrified, worrying that that Sofia might drown in a pool. But because I knew that details in a dream often represent hidden meanings and messages that need to be decoded circumstantially, I was not alarmed when I woke up but took action in my practical life as I was guided by the Spirit to correct a particular situation.

Learning to interpret dreams takes practice. It is truly like learning a new language. But the Spirit guides us in this endeavor. Listening to and learning to discern God's voice takes time. Making room for human error takes humility, and we must acknowledge it as part of the learning process. Making mistakes and learning from them is how we get better.

9 ❋ RESPONDING TO GOD'S VOICE

It was just another ordinary day in my life as a college student, and I found myself in chapel once again. Our chaplain had begun a series called "Do You Know the Plan?" Over the course of that semester he repeatedly asked us this question, convinced (even when we were not) that young college students had the intellectual capacity and spiritual acumen to offer an answer with unshakable clarity. How could I possibly know the plan God had for my life at such a young age? Was my purpose linked to my career? Was my purpose to find the right job? Was it to marry the right man? How could I possibly know what God's plan was for me? I certainly had dreams, passions, and ideas about how God might use me as my future began to unfold before me, but I truly had no idea what the big plan for my life would be.

As I began to entertain all of these thoughts, I suddenly heard a small voice say, *Christ*. Christ was to be my purpose.

At that moment the congruence of meaning completely stilled the chaos in my heart and mind. As the message drew to a close, we were invited to pick up a rock from the altar and write the plan we believed God had for us. Satisfied with the sense of direction and revelation I had received, I confidently wrote "Christ" on that little rock, knowing that from that day forward he would indeed be my plan. In a sense, Jesus is to be our aim, our goal, our *telos* in life. Of course, how we respond to his voice day in and day out has implications for the decisions we make along the pathway of life.

Saying No When God Wants Our Yes

There are moments in life when we might be tempted to run in the opposite direction of what God calls us to do. When we go through valleys of wilderness or find ourselves in situations we cannot seem to change, our first reaction might be to try to hide or run away. The pain might be too much to endure and our potential failures too much to face. This was the case of the prophet Jonah. We are given deep insight into the battles of a man of God who struggled to forgive or let God forgive those he considered his enemies. He ran from the call of God to prevent his enemies from being blessed with mercy and grace. He ran up on a mountain to wait for the judgment and destruction of the city of his enemies, and he became angry when the wrath of God did not come. The Ninevites were

known for their violence and injustice and inhuman warfare—
no wonder Jonah did not want God to forgive them!

The blatant truth is that Jonah did not want God to redeem and bless an unjust and evil people. He wanted God
to destroy them with wrath and judgment! Jonah's refusal to
obey God and respond to his call was a reflection of the state
of his own heart. He did not think it fair for God to forgive
an entire nation when they deserved to be punished for their
sins. So Jonah ran away from the Lord, setting into motion a
series of events engineered by God to bring Jonah new insight
to accomplish the mission for which he had been called. God
sent a great wind, then a storm, then a giant fish. In the depths
and distress of his soul, Jonah cried out to God for mercy and
rescue. And God did!

God rescued him out of the depths and brought him safely
to shore. As a result, Jonah had a change of *mind* but not a
change of *heart*. He decided to go to Nineveh while harboring
resentment and anger toward the people. God saw how the
Ninevites turned away from their evil ways. He had compassion and did not bring upon them the destruction he intended
to bring (Jonah 3:10). Jonah delivered the message, and God
responded with grace and compassion. But Jonah became so
angry that he desired to die because God had forgiven and
shown compassion.

The word "obedient" comes from the Latin *obedire,* which literally means to "listen to" or "pay attention to." Thus, learning to listen to the voice of God in order to follow his guidance is what true prayer is all about. Our Lord never demands our obedience, but if we are to please him, we must learn to listen. Oswald Chambers says it like this: "We have to obey him out of oneness of spirit. . . . If I hesitate it is because I love someone else in competition with him, viz., myself. Jesus Christ will not help me to obey him, I must obey him; and when I do obey him, I fulfill my spiritual destiny."[1]

I like to think about the *logic* of common sense as an appropriate description of how most people live their lives and the *illogic* of sacrificial living as one that should characterize the people of God. Rather than defending positions or identity, we ought to deny ourselves to follow God. Rather than seeking to control processes or outcomes, we must relinquish them. Rather than seeking to achieve ends, we must trust God for all outcomes. Since we are citizens of God's kingdom and it is God's Spirit who moves us, *God is responsible for the results.* This is truly important to remember because prayer is a vehicle by which God brings about what he wants to do on earth. Even though it is never manipulative, it is *effective.* So part of recog-

---

1. Oswald Chambers, *My Utmost for His Highest* (Grand Rapids: Barbour Books, 1963), November 2.

nizing the good God wants to bring about is realizing that we must be ready to obey when he speaks.

Saying No When We Need to Say No

Staying focused on our mission, calling, vision, priorities, and goals will require us to say no to certain opportunities, invitations, and requests. Setting limits help us simplify our lives and glorify God with our time, family commitments, and resources in a way that does not put us out into frantic working, deplete our energy, or make us lose sight of what matters most. After all, the little things and small distractions may cause the greatest damage. In *Stumbling on Happiness*, Daniel Gilbert brings up an interesting example. He says, "When people are asked whether they would prefer to have a job at which they earned $30,000 the first year, $40,000 the second year, and $50,000 the third year, or a job at which they earned $60,000 then $50,000 then $40,000, they generally prefer the job with the increasing wages, despite the fact that they would earn less money over the course of three years. Why would people be willing to reduce their total income in order to avoid experiencing a cut in pay?"[2] The fact is that people hate pay cuts, but research suggests that the *reason* they hate pay cuts has very little to do with the pay part and everything to do with the

---

2. Daniel Gilbert, *Stumbling on Happiness* (Toronto: Vintage Canada, 2007), 151–52.

PART III: LISTENING PRAYER

cut part. Cutting things out of our lives seems counterintuitive until we realize that if we don't cut something or say no to something we will never be able to say yes to the things God wants from us and has in store for us.

Nehemiah knew this fact well. He was serving as a cup-bearer to King Artaxerxes when news came to him that those who had survived the exile were in great trouble and disgrace because the wall of Jerusalem remained broken. As he heard about the plight of his own people his heart became sorrowful and heavy, so he sat down, mourned, prayed, and fasted. Nehemiah was blessed with a burden that became his purpose. He asked the king for permission to leave his assignment to go to Jerusalem to rebuild the wall. And he did.

When God moves us to build up his Kingdom, our spiritual enemy will try to do whatever he can to stop us. As Nehemiah was finalizing his God-given vision to rebuild the walls of Jerusalem, Sanballat and Geshem sent Nehemiah a message: "Come, let us meet together in one of the villages on the plain of Ono" (Nehemiah 6:2). Nehemiah knew they were scheming to harm him, so he essentially told them, "I am busy fulfilling the work God asked me to do! Why should I put things on hold? No, I will not stop." Nehemiah's enemies' request seemed innocent enough, but more often than not, small distractions and untimely invitations end up doing the most harm to the fulfillment of God's vision. But at other times, intimidation,

potential threats, or the fear of what could happen must be flatly rejected. Nehemiah learned this early on. Time and time again he was met with empty threats that were sent to make him stop the work, but he would not give in to fear: "Should a man like me run away? Or should someone like me go into the temple to save his life? I will not go!" (6:11). At other times he encouraged the others by telling them not to fear, turning to God through prayer day and night (4:9). Thus, as we learn to respond to the voice of God, we must commit to saying no to some things, people, and situations in order to say yes to the priorities God wants us to fulfill instead.

Saying Yes in the Waiting

Just as important as the things we wait for is what God wants to do in us while we wait. Peter compares our faith to gold, which must be refined and purified by fire (1 Peter 1:7). The waiting season is often characterized by delayed answers, and delayed answers are a type of fire. In the book *Waiting: Finding Hope When God Seems Silent*, Ben Patterson writes, "To wait on God is to see our past, especially the sins and failures of our past, as merely footprints. It says, 'This is where I was,' never, 'This is where I'm stuck. . . . To wait on God is to see our present, also, as a footprint. It says, 'This is where I am now,' never, 'This is where I must stay.'"[3] The beauty of the waiting season is that waiting seasons are never wasted times. They are preparatory and rudimentary, but they are also transitory and temporary. Granted, some waiting seasons can be long and dreadful, but, as difficult as those seasons may seem, saying yes to God often implies saying yes to waiting.

When God puts something on our hearts, it often seems out of reach because it often is. God-shaped visions are too big for us to handle. But usually in the waiting, we learn to hear the voice of God, and God shapes us in order for God's purposes to come to fruition. Did Noah have to figure out how to survive the flood on his own? Did Abraham need a road map to find the new land to which he was called? Did Joshua have to come up with his own war strategy to win the Battle of Jericho? Did David need a whole army to take down the giant Goliath? Did Moses deliver God's people as soon as he recognized they needed help? None of these heroes of the faith had everything planned, nor did they know the details, nor did they attain the promises of God as quickly as they would have liked. They learned obedience as trials came, and they often had to lean in and *relearn* obedience in the waiting.

Let's consider Moses, who perhaps once may have thought he was the most qualified and natural leader to deliver his peo-

---

3. Ben Patterson, *Waiting: Finding Hope When God Seems Silent* (Downers Grove, IL: IVP, 1989), 71.

ple out of slavery. One day, he watched the Israelites at their hard labor and became indignant when he saw an Egyptian beating a Hebrew man, so he took things into his own hands and killed that Egyptian (Exodus 2:11–12). Afterward, he fled to the wilderness, where he spent forty years tending sheep before he would be ready to deliver his people. At the end of his waiting season, God showed up in a burning bush and called him to go back to Egypt. Then Moses doubted himself, saying to God, "Who am I that I should go to Pharaoh and bring the Israelites out of Egypt?" (3:11). At first, Moses thought he could do it on his own and had enough courage to kill a man, but only after waiting in the wilderness did he develop enough discipline and the right attitude to carry out God's calling upon his life.

The good news is that, when God makes promises, he will fulfill them, but how and when are things for which we must wait. And while we wait, we develop the spiritual muscles to be patient, perseverant, and persistent along the way. But in the waiting we may also grow weary and tired. If you are going through a time of personal discouragement or are tired from the wait, don't stay there long. Get back up. Shift your perspective. Find something to do that you enjoy even in those moments when nothing around you seems to be going the way you thought life should be. Remember that God is working out his plans according to his purposes. He has not forgotten you. He is preparing you for deeper and more significant undertakings as you embrace the opportunities in front of you and keep waiting for the fulfillment of God's promises.

Saying Yes When It Might Be Costly

There will be times when responding to the voice of God will cost us something. I would like to think that responding to God would always lead to better opportunities and great success, but that is not always the case. Sometimes responding to God requires us to leave our places of comfort or privilege or familiarity. Many individuals in Scripture and throughout history can serve as examples of how costly it is to respond to the voice of God, but perhaps none equal Ruth the Moabite. After enduring a season of famine, relocating to Moab, and losing her husband and two children, Naomi was left with no clear provision. But "when Naomi heard in Moab that the LORD had come to the aid of his people by providing food for them, she and her daughters-in-law prepared to return home from there" (Ruth 1:6). Ruth refused to go back home and vowed to follow Naomi wherever she went. Ruth decided to leave the familiarity of her own country, the comfort of her own family, and venture into the unknown.

Ruth did not cling to her mother-in-law for something she wanted or needed. Ruth knew Naomi had nothing to give her. We aren't exactly sure why Ruth chose the riskier option to stay with Naomi instead of the safer option to go back to her family in Moab, but her choice makes it clear that Ruth loved Naomi a great deal. And in the end, Ruth's gain outweighed the risk because she married Boaz and became the great-grandmother of one of the greatest kings of Israel, David.

Jesus himself described the cost of the calling to those called. "'Truly I tell you,' Jesus replied, 'no one who has left home or brothers or sisters or mother or father or children or fields for me and the gospel will fail to receive a hundred times as much in this present age: homes, brothers, sisters, mothers, children and fields—along with persecutions—and in the age to come eternal life'" (Mark 10:29–30). Responding to the call may cost us a great deal. We may have to endure great trials, tribulations, and persecutions along the way. But to those who do not turn back—those who keep sowing, keep giving, keep believing, keep going, and keep saying yes despite adversity and opposition along the way—a great reversal of events is often given as a result of continual faithfulness to God.

A religious life that does not extend beyond itself but shields itself from any cost will be shackled by its own deprivations. It is not the sacrifice itself that counts. What counts is our willingness, our surrender, our love for Christ, such that even if he answers our prayer with a no, we still dare to keep saying yes to his prayers for us. Our faith is made real as we follow Christ into the crucible of the world's unrest. We can only take the first step toward true prayer when we are willing to obey the requests God makes of us along the way.

✳ CONCLUSION

There is a well-known parable attributed to Søren Kierkegaard, a renowned Danish theologian and philosopher, that goes roughly something like this:

It was a lovely Sunday morning. And, like every Sunday, all the ducks got ready to go to duck church, waddling through the doors and down the aisles and into the pews, where they comfortably sat in their normal places. When all were well settled and the hymns were sung, the minister waddled into the pulpit and opened the duck Bible and began to read: "Hear ye, oh ducks, the word of the Lord! Ducks, you have wings, and with wings you can fly like eagles! You can soar into the sky! Ducks, you can escape the confinement of fences and know the joy of absolute freedom! Ducks, use your wings and fly!" It was a marvelous and inspiring scripture, and all the ducks nodded and said in unison, "Amen! Hallelujah!" They recognized the power of the words and the promises they could attain by applying what they heard. But when the benediction was given, they got up from their pews and, one by one, walked out the door of the church, waddling through town all the way home. We have been made to soar on wings like eagles. We have been made to jump over obstacles with feet like the deer. But most of us keep waddling instead of flying because we have not learned that prayer is the way by which we can turn on the engine of our spirit and start flying high and jumping over the obstacles of life! We, like the ducks, recognize the power and promise of prayer. We all affirm we need it. We all know we should engage in it. We all agree it's a wonderful thing. But doing it is just so difficult at times, so we go on through life waddling instead. But the invitation of prayer is to come with no pretense and to instead lay our souls bare before the living God and allow him to transform us.

Prayer reveals the need and the emptiness of the requester while inviting us to rest on the provision and plentitude of the One who hears us. We might feel inadequate when we pray—that's okay! Prayer is truly an invitation to come as we are, recognizing that it is never too late to learn and to change.

If it wasn't too late for a rebel named Eve who became the mother of creation, then it's never too late!

If it wasn't too late for a barren woman named Sarah whose descendants became as numerous as the sands on the seashore, then it's never too late!

If it wasn't too late for a deceiver named Jacob who became the father of God's chosen people, then it's never too late!

If it wasn't too late for a murderer named Moses who led God's people out of slavery in Egypt, then it's never too late!

If it wasn't too late for an adulterer named David who became a man after God's own heart, then it's never too late!

If it wasn't too late for a coward named Peter who became the leader of Christ's church, then it's never too late!

If it wasn't too late for a persecutor and murderer named Paul who became the greatest missionary in the history of Christianity, then it's never too late!

We can start again. We can start fresh. We can start over. We can pick up right where we left off. We can come just as we are and allow the power of prayer to change us one step at a time, knowing that God is right there with us, beckoning us to come empty-handed, vulnerable, and naked so we may be filled, blessed, saturated, and covered by his ever-increasing and everlasting grace.

Life on earth is but a short pilgrimage, and it would be wise for us to learn to travel light. One way is to let go of the bitterness, the piled-up hurts, the unmet expectations, and invite God to refresh us. Because prayer at its most essential level is *relational,* we learn how to connect with God with the intent to know him more intimately. Because prayer at its primal level is *positional,* it affords us the opportunity to approach the throne of God with full confidence that he hears us because we are heirs of his kingdom. Because prayer at the unseen level is *situational*, we can come to God just as we are while knowing he will not leave us there. He will hear our prayers, receive them, and in due time answer them in the best way, giving us great anticipation for today and bright hope for tomorrow.